SWANSEA DOCKS
IN THE 1960S

SWANSEA DOCKS IN THE 1960S

MARK LEE INMAN

AMBERLEY

To Freddy and Alexa, two wonderful grandchildren.

First published 2017

Amberley Publishing
The Hill, Stroud
Gloucestershire, GL5 4EP

www.amberley-books.com

British Library Cataloguing in Publication Data.
A catalogue record for this book is available from the British Library.

ISBN 978 1 4456 6592 4 (print)
ISBN 978 1 4456 6593 1 (ebook)

Typeset in 10pt on 13pt Sabon.
Origination by Amberley Publishing.
Printed in the UK.

Contents

Introduction

I spent my childhood and teenage years living near the Mumbles in South Wales. My bedroom overlooked Swansea Bay and from my earliest childhood the passage of ships in and out of Swansea Docks was a continual fascination.

After much badgering, in late 1962 the British Transport Docks Board granted me a permit to enter the docks and take photographs of any ships that were berthed. As a result, over the next few years I was able to capture what was to prove the swan song of the traditional cargo liner and tramp steamer.

It was a transition period. It was still possible to see elderly, weather-worn war standards and even, occasionally, ships from the pre-war era. Many dated from the period of post-war reconstruction while, as the 1960s progressed, newer, bigger and faster ships were appearing. Ships of the famous companies such as Alfred Holt's Blue Funnel Line, Ellerman Line and Clan Line appeared on a regular basis. The container revolution meant bigger ships, fewer ships and the end of traditional cargo liners coasting around to collect their various cargoes. It also meant faster turnarounds.

One of the interesting features of this coasting round for cargoes was that ships would often arrive in ballast to load tinplate as the bottom cargo. Other cargoes would then be loaded at either Liverpool or London prior to embarking on the next voyage. The Blue Funnel liners were the classic examples of this. Arriving in Liverpool from the Far East to unload, they would coast round with latex to Swansea before returning to Liverpool with their bottom cargo of tinplate. This would create the strange image of a ship riding fairly high in the water both when coming in and going out.

The container revolution, still only on the horizon in the early to mid-1960s, did not happen overnight. Many of the ports that traditional ships served were much slower to adapt to container handling. The revolution demanded major changes in both ships and harbour facilities. As a result, many of the ships depicted survived with their original owners well into the late 1970s and beyond. Others eked out a less glamorous life under dubious foreign flags. This book captures those last few years.

Where possible, I have researched what happened to the ships and their owners in subsequent years. Some ships had quite eventful careers, while others went about their lawful occasions well out of the limelight. As a result, the length of caption and amount of detail will vary enormously.

In conducting my research, I have to acknowledge the help from George Gunn's *White Funnel Memories*, C. H. Milsom's *Blue Funnel – The Later Years*, Ambrose Greenaway's

Cargo Liners, Andrew Wiltshire's *Looking Back at Traditional Cargo Liners*, two editions of Bert Moody's *Ocean Ships*, H. M. Le Fleming's *Ships of the Holland-America Line*, Laurence Dunn's *Ships of the Union-Castle Line*, and Mitchell and Sawyer's three excellent volumes on the wartime Empire, Ocean, Forts and Parks, and the Liberty ships. Debt is also owed to the many shipping company, shipbuilding and ship-spotting websites. Special thanks must be given to W. 'Bill' Moore of the local branch of the World Ships Society for his help on the more recent history of Swansea Docks. However, any mistakes or misinterpretations are down to me.

For the photographic technical, most of the pictures are in black and white. Until October 1964 I was still using a Brownie Box camera when the shiny new 35 mm Voigtlender Vito C with its fine Color-Skopar lens came on stream. Even then, it was a while before I had a light metre and could reliably take colour photographs. For the technical, most of the black and white pictures use Ilford FP3 film. Colour was usually Kodakchrome or Kodakcolour.

Again I must acknowledge the debt to my ever-tolerant and gracious wife, who listened patiently to progress reports and scanned the final proofs. Connor Stait and his team are owed a huge debt for their encouragement but also gracious tolerance of my totally inadequate knowledge of the demands of the twenty-first-century publishing industry.

A Brief History of Swansea Docks

Inevitably, a port in South Wales is going to be associated with the movement of coal. In addition, in the early eighteenth century there was iron production along with copper smelting and tinplate manufacture, which required the establishment of wharves along the banks of the River Tawe.

Trade increased throughout the eighteenth century, requiring the development of more permanent harbour facilities. In 1791, the Swansea Harbour Trust was founded to undertake this development. The first task was to widen and deepen the channel to allow access for the larger trading vessels of the day. Navigation was improved with the establishment of the Mumbles lighthouse in 1791 and by 1809 the work to build two stone breakwaters to enclose and protect the river entrance was completed.

By this time the port had been linked to the collieries and smelting works by the Swansea Canal, which connected the port to Ystradgynlais 18 miles up the Tawe Valley. A further link was provided by the Tennant Canal, which provided a link between the Neath Canal at Aberdulais and Port Tennant in the neighbouring Fabian's Bay area.

Industrial development, particularly of non-ferrous metal processing during the eighteenth century, had led to Swansea becoming a world leader in the business of metallurgical processing and manufacture. This industrial expansion demanded larger and better port facilities and Swansea Harbour Trust developed the North Dock by diverting the lower reach of the River Tawe into a new cut and turning the former riverbed into an enclosed dock. This work was completed in 1852. In that same year, a private concern – the Swansea Dock Company – had begun constructing a second enclosed dock, the South Dock, on the west bank and foreshore of the River Tawe. However, financial difficulties set in and the Swansea Harbour Trust bought up the Swansea Dock Company, completing the project in 1859.

By 1870 the port was handling over 1.5 million tons of cargo per annum and in 1877 it was recorded that no other harbour in the kingdom was handling so much cargo in such a limited amount of space. The demand for further facilities was such that in 1879 the Swansea Harbour Trust began the construction of a new enclosed dock on the east side of the River Tawe, taking in the whole of Fabian's Bay. This dock, the Prince of Wales, was completed in 1881. It was formally opened by the Prince and Princess of Wales in 1882 and further enlarged in 1898. A full network of rail links and sidings were provided to bring the coal to the numerous loading hoists.

The copper trade declined sharply towards the end of the nineteenth century, but this was compensated by growth in coal exports, which were running at over 2 million tons per annum. In the last quarter of the nineteenth century tinplate exports grew from 6,000 tons to over 250,000 by 1895. This latter product was to become one of Swansea Docks' major traffic flows.

To cater for the increased traffic, construction of a new and larger dock was commenced in 1905 on the seaward side of the Prince of Wales Dock. This dock, the King's Dock, was completed in 1909 along with a long breakwater to enclose a large area of water, which eventually became known as the Queen's Dock, opened officially in 1920.

With the King's Dock in operation, the export of coal and related products reached the record figure of 5.5 million tons in 1913. Tinplate exports peaked at 621,000 tons in 1924. However, there were changes. The early twentieth century saw the move away from coal to oil and the first oil refinery to be built in the United Kingdom was completed nearby at Llandarcy (a totally hybrid name!) and opened in 1922. This created a demand for oil-handling facilities in the Queen's Dock and by the 1950s some 8 million tons of petroleum products was being shipped in or out through Swansea.

Contemporary with this expansion, the dock facilities on the west side of the river became obsolete. The North Dock was closed in 1930 and largely filled in, leaving just a basin, which remained open until 1969. The South Dock closed in 1971 and was redeveloped as a marina and the prestigious Maritime Quarter.

The post-war decline in coal traffic has led to the running-down of the Prince of Wales Dock, which is now part of the SA1 redevelopment scheme featuring commercial buildings, leisure and academic facilities, as well as housing. There are plans to construct a new tidal entrance to provide berths for 400 boats in a new marina. Only the King's Dock remains operational. The trend towards container ships – bigger ships visiting fewer ports – led to a general decline from the late 1960s. The port is now very much a backwater, only handling coastal traffic with vessels of 6,000 dwt or larger becoming very rare sights. Meanwhile, the Queen's Dock, now devoid of oil traffic because of the closure of the Llandarcy and the nearby Baglan Bay chemical plant refinery, has become a major mussel-producing area, supplying prestigious up-market restaurants in the area with delicious locally reared mussels. However, the long breakwater on the seaward side of the dock will form the landward side of the new £1.3 billion tidal lagoon electricity generation project, which was announced in January 2017.

Our journey will start with the Prince of Wales Dock, then move into the King's Dock and finally to the Queen's Dock. Where there are a large number of photographs of ships from the same line, they will be grouped together. Single shots will follow in a grouped miscellany.

Prince of Wales Dock Miscellany

Egee, 1940, 2,667 tons, Soc. Navale Caennaise, France

Welsh ports are traditionally associated with the export of coal. By the 1960s, the coal trade was in terminal decline, but there were still regular movements. The local *Evening Post* reported daily how many dock workers had been employed and how much coal, usually anthracite for France, had been shipped. It was a rare action shot, so I could not resist it. The ship was on her way out of the Prince of Wales Dock to the main lock and the open sea.

She was a humble collier, but she had an impressive history. Built by Ateliers & Chantiers de la Seine in 1940, she either escaped or was seized in 1940 to serve under the British government for the duration of the war. She was returned to her French owners in 1945 and remained with them until 1964. Obviously, when this photograph was taken, she was near the end of her service with her French owners. Sold in 1964, she sailed under the Liberian flag until 1967 when she was sold again to Greek interests. In September 1968, while en route from Archangel to Sharpness with a cargo of timber, she was wrecked on rocks off the Isle of Islay in the Inner Hebrides.

Commandant Le Terrier, 1947, 2,617 tons, France
A classic picture of a collier loading under the hoist. Although French, she was built in Grangemouth and sold to Liberia in 1964 and then on to Panamanian interests to become the *Konstatinos* in 1968. Grounded in 1969, she became a constructive total loss.

SNA 5
Little is known about this particular ship, caught waiting to load coal in the Prince of Wales Dock. 'SNA' stands for Soc. Nationale d'Affretements. This company owes its origin to the French PLM railway company, who established it to import coal from the UK (probably Wales) for its locomotives. The company was still extant when this picture was taken and the original house flag – a white flag with a blue star – can be seen on the funnel.

Sottteville, 1948, Soc. Nationale d'Affretements, France
Another action shot, full and down, steaming away from the Prince of Wales Dock towards the main dock exit. Built by the Burrard Dry Dock Company in Vancouver, BC, she was originally the *SNA 7*.

Irish Fir, 1956, Irish Shipping, Eire
Irish Shipping Limited was set up in 1941 as a war-time expediency. After a post-war period of growth and success, there were twenty ships in the fleet by 1960. Difficulties in the early 1960s led to some fleet rationalisation, but confidence and optimism returned by the end of the decade. New ships were ordered and commissioned, but a further downturn in the early 1980s sadly resulted in the company being liquidated in November 1984.

This has to be a classic picture of a coaster waiting in the Prince of Wales Dock to load coal for Ireland. One of three small sister ships designed initially to trade to the Baltic, she eventually traded far and wide across the Atlantic to both South and North America, even reaching Hudson's Bay in northern Canada. She was sold in 1969.

Above: *Stalheim*, Norway
A classic picture of a Norwegian collier loading coal in the Prince of Wales Dock.
Coincidently, a previous *Stalheim*, owned by the same company, sank after striking a magnetic mine while leaving nearby Port Talbot docks, also with a cargo of coal, on 31 July 1940.

Opposite above: *Jnga Bastian,* 1958, 1,542 tons, Helmut Bastian, Germany
Built by Abeking & Rusmessen at Lemwerder, Lower Saxony, Germany, she was lengthened in 1959 and re-engined in 1965. She became the French *Marie Louise* in 1972 and the Greek *Crusader* in 1978. She was laid up in 1980 but returned to trading in 1984 as the *Eolos,* remaining under the Greek flag. She was eventually broken up at Aliaga in 2009.

Opposite below: *Lyminge*, 1967, 4,816 tons
Built by Caledon, Dundee, and judging by the approximate date of this photograph, she must have been quite new, certainly less than a year old. A classic Welsh ports picture – loading coal at the hoist in the Prince of Wales Dock.

The ship became the Jugoslav *Krapanj* in 1975, in 1989 the Maltese *Rapan* and in 1994 *Pan*, still under the Maltese flag. In February 1996 she grounded near Gibraltar about 20 miles east of Europa Point and she was broken up in situ.

King's Dock

Bibby Line

The Liverpool-based Bibby Line started as coastal traders in 1801. The company still exists, trading from Douglas, Isle of Man, and the familiar clenched-fist-held dagger emblem can still be seen. It is the oldest family-controlled company in the UK.

Leicestershire, 1949, 8,922 tons

Built by Fairfields, she was the last passenger ship delivered to Bibby Line. It was rare to see a genuine passenger ship in Swansea, especially one fitted out to carry seventy-six first class passengers in relative luxury.

In 1964, not long after this photograph was taken, she was sold to the Greek Typaldos Line who converted her into a ro-ro and renamed her *Herakion*. In December 1966, while en route from Canea to Piraeus, she capsized and sank with the loss of 217 lives after a lorry broke loose and smashed through a side door in bad weather.

Gloucestershire (ex-*Cingalese Prince*, ex-*Gallic*, ex-*Cingalese Prince*), 1950, 8,808 tons
Another example of a ship transferred between different parts of a major group. Again, after starting life with the Prince Line she was transferred in 1960 to Shaw Savill but returned to Prince Line in 1962.

Sold to Cypriot interests in 1971, she was eventually broken up in Shanghai in 1974.

Staffordshire (ex-*Bardic*, ex-*Eastern Prince*), 1950, 8,808 tons
The Bibby Line ships were named for English shires. Built by Vickers Armstrong on the Tyne, this ship had started life with the Furness Withy Prince Line and moved within the group to the Shaw Savill Line before becoming the *Staffordshire* in 1964. She was scrapped in Hong Kong in 1971.

Blue Funnel (Alfred Holt & Co.)

Alfred Holt's Blue Funnel Line was founded in Liverpool in 1865. They traded from Glasgow, Liverpool and Swansea to China and Japan, the Malay Peninsula and the Dutch East Indies. Services to Australia began in 1889 and, to compete against Dutch companies on the east coast of Sumatra, a Dutch subsidiary – Nederlandsche Stoomvaart Maatschappij 'Oceaan' (NSMO) – was established in 1891. From the very earliest years, the ships were regular, almost weekly visitors to Swansea, bringing in latex and loading tinplate as bottom cargo. The characteristic vertical blue funnel was very conspicuous if one looked across Swansea Bay towards the docks when one was in port. A substantial player in the liner cargo trade, the fleet consisted of over seventy ships, amounting to over 470,000 gross tons in the mid-1960s. This total excludes the Glen Line and Elder Dempster Line fleets, which were also part of the Holt empire. The onset of the container revolution meant that most of the fleet was sold or scrapped during the 1970s. Few of the traditional Blue Funnel ships survived into the 1980s.

Pyrrhus, 1949, 10,093 tons
Built by Cammell Laird, she was one of four Perseus-class ships similar in size to the contemporary Helenus class. The larger Blue Funnel ships were rare visitors to Swansea. She suffered a major fire while in the Liverpool Huskisson Dock in November 1964 and was sold for scrapping in Taiwan in September 1972.

Astynax (ex-*Glenfruin*), 1948, 8,319 tons
Astynax was built by Scotts of Greenock and transferred in 1957 to Glen Line, becoming the *Glenfruin*. She was returned to Blue Funnel in 1962 and reverted to her original name. In December 1972 she was sold for breaking up at Kaohsiung.

Memnon, 1959, 8,504 tons
Built by Vickers Armstrongs at Newcastle, she was one of a batch of six 8,000 gross ton M-class ships built at the end of the 1950s. They were the last Blue Funnel ships to have the traditional vertical funnel and masts. In 1975 she was renamed *Stentor* prior to being transferred to the Elder Dempster Line as the *Owerri*. She was sold to a Greek operator in 1978 and was reported laid up at Stylis in 1982. In 1987 she was transferred to the Maltese flag and was scrapped in India in 1988. As such, she was the last of the Menetheus class to be scrapped, and the last of the traditional Blue Funnel ships.

This photograph was taken during the harsh winter of early 1963. Snow can be seen on the warehouse roof and slush on the key.

For the photographic technical, I was still using my Kodak 620 Box Brownie at the time.

Aeneas, 1947, 8,295 tons
One of the many Anchises-class Blue Funnel ships built as part of the post-war rebuilding. She was built by Caledon, Dundee, and was sold for scrapping in Taiwan in 1972.

Blue Funnel ships were a regular sight; their large vertical funnels and distinctive livery made them very conspicuous. Almost every week one would arrive to discharge latex and load tinplate as bottom cargo. They almost invariably berthed in the King's Dock at 'A' shed.

Calchas, 1947, 7,631 tons
Almost an action shot. The ship is seen locking out at the start of her voyage.

Another Anchises-class ship, but built by Harland & Wolff, she spent some time sailing for Glen Line as the *Glenfinlas*. Returned to Blue Funnel in 1962, she was briefly transferred to Elder Dempster Line in 1971. She was gutted by fire off Port Kelang in July 1973 and was subsequently towed to Kaohsiung to be broken up.

Elpenor, 1954, 7,757 tons
High summer in 1963 and the *Elpenor* waits to lock into the docks. Built by Harland & Wolff, she was transferred to Elder Dempster Lines in 1976. In 1977 she was sold to Liberian interests to become the *United Concorde*, flying the Panamanian flag, and was sold for breaking up in Taiwan in August 1979.

Melampus, 1960, 8,511 tons
Built by Vickers Armstrong, Newcastle, she was one of a batch of six M-class ships. In 1967 she became trapped in the Bitter Lake and was declared a constructive total loss in February 1969. In 1975 she was sold to the Grecomar Shipping Agency of Piraeus and was towed out of the canal to discharge her cargo in Trieste. In 1976 she was renamed *Annoula II* and was broken up in Karachi in 1983.

Myrmidon (ex-*Ripon Victory*), 1945, 7,715 tons
Laid down on 25 May 1945 at the yard of Permanente Metals Corporation in Richmond (California), she was completed and delivered eighty-eight days later on 21 August. She was acquired by Blue Funnel in 1947. After twenty-six years of service she was sold to Taiwanese interests for breaking up in 1971 and was transferred to Elder Dempster Line for the final delivery voyage.

Sarpedon (ex-*Denbighshire*), 1939, 8,790 tons
The transfer from Glen Line had not long taken place when this picture was taken. She still sported a Glen Line red funnel. One of the fast, modern cargo liners ordered by Glen Line from the Netherlands, she served with great distinction during the Second World War on the Malta convoys, both in convoy but also on lone runs because of her speed. She also served in the Pacific theatre in 1945. She was transferred to Blue Funnel in 1967 and was sold for scrapping in Taiwan in 1969. She was the longest serving Glen Line ship.

Anchises, 1947, 7,634 tons

The *Anchises* herself. Built by Caledon, Dundee, in June 1949 for Ocean Steamship, she was bombed by Chinese Nationalist aircraft in the Whangpo River while en route for Shanghai. Badly damaged, she settled by the stern in shallow water and survived a second unsuccessful attack. Repaired and re-floated, she was towed into Shanghai to discharge her cargo before being towed to Kobe, Japan, for repair.

In 1973 she was transferred within the group to NSM Oceaan, becoming the *Alcinous*. A year later she was transferred twice, first to Glen Line then back to Ocean Steamship.

She was sold for scrapping in Kaohsiung in 1975.

Tantalus (ex-*Macmurray* Victory), 1945, 7,674 tons

Tantalus was built by Permante Metals Corporation at Richmond (CA). It reflects the lessening sense of urgency that it took 100 days from keel laying in March 1945 to delivery at the end of June. Bought in 1946 by Blue Funnel, she was allocated to NSM Oceaan and given the name *Polyphemus*. In June 1960 she was transferred to Blue Funnel's Ocean Steam as the *Tantalus*. In 1969, after a period laid up in the River Fal, she was sold to Panamanina interests for scrapping. Her final voyage, with a cargo of scrap, was to Kaohsiung under the name *Pelops*.

Rhexenor, 1945, 10,199 tons
Originally laid down by Caledon of Dundee as one of the fast 'Empire Life' ships for the Ministry of War Transport, she was bought on the stocks by Blue Funnel and completed to company specification. She was sold for scrapping in May 1975 and was broken up at Kaohsiung.

Stentor, 1946, 10,192 tons
Ordered as one of the Ministry of War Transport's Empire Life cargo ships, she was delivered directly to Blue Funnel. Between 1958 and 1963 she was with Glen Line as the *Glenshiel*. She was transferred to Elder Dempster Line in 1973 and sold for scrapping in Taiwan in 1975.

Ulysses, 1949, 8,976 tons
Another almost-action-shot as she locks out at the start of her voyage.

Ordered from J. L. Thompson of Sunderland by Silver Line as the *Silverholly,* she was bought on the stocks and delivered to Blue Funnel as the *Ulysses.* She was allocated to the Blue Funnel operating company China Mutual Steam Navigation and thus lived up to the appellation given by the Swansea dockers as a 'China Boat'.

She was sold to Greek buyers in 1971 and was scrapped in Shanghai in 1974.

Laertes, 1949, 8,270 tons, (NSMO) Netherlands
Built by Vickers Armstrong at Newcastle upon Tyne, in March 1972 she transferred to Elder Dempster Line but retained her Dutch registry. Later in the year she transferred to the China Mutual Steam Navigation operating company, becoming the *Idomeneus* and flying the red duster. After spending time on charter to both Elder Dempster Lines and Nigerian National Line, she was sold in 1976 to Gulf Lines and renamed *Gulf Voyager.* She was sold for scrap in 1978 and was broken up at Gadani Beach.

Above: *Menestheus*, 1958, 8,510 tons
Also built by Caledon of Dundee, *Menestheus* was also transferred to Elder Dempster Line in 1977, becoming the *Onitsha*. Like the *Machaon*, she was sold to Greek buyers, becoming the *El Island* under the Cypriot flag. She was broken up at Kaohsiung in 1979.

Opposite above: *Lycaon*, 1954, 7,835 tons, (NSMO) Netherlands
Doubtless in order to facilitate ease of trading in the former Dutch East Indies, in 1895 Blue Funnel set up a Dutch subsidiary operating company (N. S. M. Oceaan). Ships allocated to this company flew the Netherlands flag and were registered in Rotterdam.

The *Lycaon* was built by Vickers Armstrong and transferred to NSMO in 1960. In 1975 she was transferred to Elder Dempster Line without a change of name, but was painted in EDL colours. She returned to Blue Funnel in 1976 as the *Glaucus* and in 1977 was sold to a Liberian company to become the *United Vanguard*, flying the Singapore flag.

In May 1979, while en route from Sharjah to Bassein on the Irrawaddy delta, she suffered a major engine failure caused by the fracture of a sea water cooling pipe and had to be abandoned.

Opposite below: *Adrastus*, 1953, 7,859 tons, (NSMO) Netherlands
Built by Vickers Armstrong, she was transferred to NSMO in 1960 and was then transferred in 1975 to Elder Demspter Line, acquiring the buff funnel but no change of name. In 1978 she was sold to Cypriot interests and was eventually broken up at Gadani Beach in 1981.

This photograph is unusual because the ship is berthed at the Graig Ola wharf on the south side of King's Dock.

Machaon, 1959, 8530 tons
The six Menetheus-class ships were built in the late 1950s. They were slightly longer, bigger and marginally faster than the earlier Anchises class. They were also the last Blue Funnel ships to have the classic vertical funnel profile.

Built by Caledon, Dundee, she was transferred to NSM Oceaan in 1970 and in 1977 to Elder Dempster Line, becoming the *Obuasi*. She was sold to Greek buyers in 1978, becoming the *El Sea* under the Cypriot flag. Later the same year she became the Liberian *Med Endeavour* and was sold for breaking up at Kaohsiung in 1979.

Maron, 1960, 8,531 tons
Another Menestheus-class ship, also built by Caledon of Dundee, and operated by Ocean Steam Ship. In 1975 she was transferred to the China Mutual Steam Navigation company, taking the name *Rhexenor*. In 1977 she was transferred to the Elder Dempster Line and became the *Opobo*. She was sold to Greek buyers in 1978 and was later operated as the Liberian *Europe II*. Laid up in Pireaus in 1982, she was sold in 1984 to Maltese buyers and was then sold on for scrap and broken up at Aliaga in Turkey in 1987.

Protesilaus, 1967, 12,094 tons

One of eight larger and faster (21 knots) ships ordered by the Blue Funnel group – four were allocated to Glen Line and four to Blue Funnel's Ocean Steamship operating company. Eventually, the four Glen Line ships were transferred to Blue Funnel and given Blue Funnel names. Despite the problems with British shipbuilding at the time, only two of the ships were built in Japan.

The *Protesilaus* was built by Vickers at Newcastle and along with the three sisters sold to C. Y. Tung, Hong Kong, becoming the *Oriental Importer.* Following damage arising from a rocket attack in the Arabian Gulf in June 1985, she was sold for scrap and broken up in Kaohsiung.

The difference in size is noticeable. At 50 feet longer than the earlier Helenus and Perseus-class ships, in the constricted environment of a dock area it is quite a squeeze into the frame without falling into the water.

Although I saw and photographed all four Glen Line ships, the *Protesilaus* was the only one of the four ships initially allocated to Blue Funnel that I ever saw.

Coincidently, in January 1940, the previous *Protesilaus* was mined in the Bristol Channel and abandoned in a sinking condition. While under tow she ran aground near the Mumbles lighthouse. Eventually re-floated, she was so badly damaged that she was sold for scrap and was broken up in nearby Briton Ferry in 1942.

Bristol City Line

Charles Hill's Bristol City Line originally dated from 1704. The steamship service to New York started in 1879. There was also a Canadian service, which was extended to the Great Lakes in 1958. As a result, the ships trading between Europe and North America were a regular sight, virtually operating a liner service. Bristol City Line did move into the container era in 1970 but the company and its container ships were taken over by Bibby Line in 1971 and the company ceased trading in 1974.

Above: *Bristol City*, 1959, 5,887 tons
The *Bristol City* was built by Redhead at South Shields. She was sold to Panamanian interests in 1970 and became the *Agelos Gabriel*. She was scrapped in Split (Croatia) in April 1980.

Opposite above: *New York City*, 1956, 5,603 tons
Another Redhead-built ship, she was sold in 1968 to become the Gibraltar-registered *Avis Ornis*. Sold on to Cypriot interests she become the *Felicity*, before being sold again to the People's Republic of China.
   She and the *Bristol City* were the last of the pre-1960-built ships.
   (Not long after she was sold I photographed her in the West India Docks, London, still sporting the Bristol City Line star on her bow.)

Opposite below: *Montreal City*, 1963, 6,623 tons
An early-morning action shot. The ship has just come through the lock from the sea into the King's Dock. She was built at Burntisland in Fife and appears to be sporting the traditional black hull with the company name along the side. Although modern in looks, Bristol City Line moved into containerisation at the end of the 1960s and she was sold to Thailand to become the *Ratchaburi*. She was lost as the result of fire off the Thai coast in March 1973.

Gloucester City, 1954, 5,581 tons
Gloucester City was built by Redhead at South Shields. It seems the older ships in the Bristol City Line fleet lost the company name from the side of the hull. In 1968 she was sold to Panamanian interests to become the *St John* but in October 1968 she was wrecked off Fort Dauphin in Madagascar while en route from Montreal to Djakarta.

Halifax City, 1964, 6,647 tons
One of the changes brought by the 1960s was the replacement of the black hull by an orange one, although Bert Moody called it red. Perhaps vermillion might be an acceptable compromise. The practice of painting the company name alongside the hull was also replaced by painting it on the superstructure.

The *Halifax City* was built at Burntisland and was sold in 1972 to Thailand to become the *Thornburi* and then the *Nakornthon*.

Brocklebank Line

Brocklebank Line originally dated from 1801 as a coastal coal trader operating out of Whitehaven. It expanded into the Indian trade in 1813 following the cessation of the East India Company monopoly. Later treaties in the mid-nineteenth century enabled the company to expand operations into China. Liverpool became the terminal port in 1819. Curiously, the company did not build its first steamship until 1889. The Cunard interest dated from 1911, when shares were acquired. Cunard-Brocklebank was eventually formed in 1968 with a pooling of all cargo ships. Some Cunarders even gained traditional Brocklebank Indian 'Ma' names. However, containerisation and financial losses meant that the company ceased to exist by 1983.

Mangla, 1959, 8,805 tons
One of the five-ship Masirah class built by William Hamilton at Port Glasgow between 1957 and 1960, she is receiving attention in the Palmer's Dry Dock. In 1968 the independent Brocklebank Line became Cunard-Brocklebank and in 1972 the *Mangla* was sold to the Greek Marchessini Lines to become the *Eurypylus*. Following an engine room explosion off the Californian coast in 1975, she was scrapped at Kaohsiung in 1976.

Makrana, 1957, 8,764 tons
Another of the Masirah class built by William Hamilton. Following the merger into Cunard she was sold in 1971 to Greece to become the *Aegis Glory* and later *Aegis Eternity,* only to then be scrapped in Shanghai in 1974.

Maskeliya, 1954, 7,350 tons
Slightly smaller than the Masirah-class ships but also built by William Hamilton, she was sold to Hong Kong buyers in 1969, becoming the *Ocean Joy,* and was dispatched to Kaohsiung for breaking up in 1972.

Burma Five Star Line Burma (Myanmar)

Burma Five Star Line was established in 1959 as the state-controlled deep sea shipping fleet of Burma. Political changes in 1990 led to the company being renamed Myanmar Five Star Line.

Bassein, 1963, 7,435 tons
The *Bassein* was one of two sister ships delivered in 1963 from A. G. Weser in Bremerhaven. Two more sisters were built in Japan. Doubtlessly to be rid of any colonial associations, she was renamed *Pathein* in 1989.

Mergui, 1963, 7,458 tons
One of two sisters built in Japan by the Uraga Dock. She survived a fire in Avonmouth docks in May 1973 and was renamed *Myeik* in 2002 and broken up in Myanmar in late 2003.

Clan Line

The Clan Line was founded in Liverpool in 1877 by Charles Cayzer and traded between the UK and India via the Suez Canal. It became Clan Line in 1881. In the 1950s, Clan Line was merged with Union Castle to form British & Commonwealth Shipping Limited. The group moved away from shipping into financial services. Clan Line effectively ceased to exist in 1981.

Above: Clan MacGowan, 1963, 9,039 tons
One of three sisters built at Greenock Dockyard, notable for the fact that they pioneered remote control of the main engine room from a desk in a separate control room for British ships. I am reliably informed that the problem chief engineers had with such an arrangement was assembling a foursome for Bridge! She was sold in 1970 to become the *Indian Tribune* and was broken up in Calcutta in 1985.

On her deck can be seen part of a consignment of locomotives from English Electric being delivered to what was then Rhodesian Railways.

Opposite above: Clan Urquhart, 1943, 9,726 tons
Built by Greenock Dockyard and despite the date was not allocated an 'Empire' name. She was broken up in Taiwan in 1966, so this must be a photograph from when she was close to the end of her days. It is also unusual because she is berthed at the Graig Ola wharf.

Opposite below: Clan Finlay, 1962, 9,262 tons
One of the modern three-quarter aft Ferguson quintet. Built by Swan Hunter at Wallsend, she was sold in 1968 to the Iranian Arya National Shipping Corporation of Khorramshar and renamed *Ayra Far*. She was sold again in 1971 to Somali interests to become the *Atlantic Ocean* and on to Chinese interests in 1975 to become the *Lu Chun*. She was broken up in China in 1992.

Clan Macgregor, 1962, 9,059
One of three sisters built by Greenock Dockyard that pioneered remote-control engine rooms. In 1981 she was sold to Greece to become the *Angelikar*. In 1982 she caught fire some 60 miles south-east of Cyprus. Towed first to Larnaca Roads and then to Piraeus for disposal, she was broken up in Greece in 1983.

Clan Mactaggart, 1949, 8,035 tons
Built by Greenock Dockyard, she served Clan Line until broken up in Spain in November 1971.

Clan Stewart, 1954, 8,564 tons
Built at Greenock on the Clyde, she was the first of a second batch of similar vessels ordered by Clan Line and Pacific Steam Navigation. Briefly transferred to what became Safmarine in 1961, she was returned to Clan Line and operated as the Union Castle *Kinpurnie Castle*. She was sold in 1967 to become the Panamanian-flagged *Hellenic Med* and was broken up at Gadani Beach in 1978.

Clan MacTavish, 1949, 8,035 tons
Built by Greenock Dockyard in 1949, she was scrapped at Whampoa, China, in 1971.
   She is moored at the next berth along from the *Clan Stewart* above in much better weather.

King Malcolm, 1952, 5,883 tons, King Line
Another shot in the bitterly cold, prolonged winter of 1962/63. The snow can be seen on the roof of the transit shed.

One of three sisters built by Harland & Wolff in Belfast. She was sold to Greece in 1972 to become the *Kanaris* and in 1980 became the *Dimitra K.* Laid up at Chittagong in 1981, she was eventually beached at Faujderhat Beach in July 1983 for breaking up.

The King Line was a wholly owned subsidiary of Union Castle acquired in 1948.

Clan Ranald, 1965, 10,541 tons
Actually owned by Union Castle Line, she was effectively one of their R-class refrigerated ships. She had been originally ordered by Union Castle from Greenock Dockyard. She became the *Dover Castle* in 1977 and *Dover Universal* in 1979. Sold to become the Greek-registered *Golden Sea* in 1981, she was broken up at Gadani Beach in 1985.

Above: *Clan Brodie*, 1941, 7,473 tons
Built at Greenock Dockyard, she was
taken over on the stocks by the Royal
Navy and converted to the aircraft
transport auxiliary HMS *Athene*.
Returned to Clan line in 1946, she was
scrapped in Hong Kong in June 1963.
This photograph must have been taken
in the last year of her life.

Right: *King David*, (ex-*Empire Mist*),
1941, 7,251 tons, Bullard & King Line
Built by Doxfords of Sunderland for
the Ministry of War Transport as the
Empire Mist, she was purchased by
King Line in 1945. King Line was
taken over by Union Castle in 1949
and then became part of British &
Commonwealth Shipping in 1956. The
ship was sold in 1962, not long after
this picture was taken, to become the
Liberian *Hong Kong Venture* and was
sold again in 1966 without a change
of flag or name. She was scrapped in
Hong Kong in 1969.

Cunard Line

Cunard Line was originally formed by the Cunard brothers in 1838. It was awarded a transatlantic mail contract in 1839 and began to be associated with a regular transatlantic passenger liner service. Over the years many of the liners were household names and regular holders of the prestigious Blue Riband. There was also a cargo side and in the mid-1960s the main Cunard fleet consisted of nine cargo liners. Container ships were operated from 1969 and the company became part of the Trafalgar House group on 1971. Only the passenger business remains under the Cunard brand and since 1998 it has been part of the Carnival Corporation.

Phrygia, 1955, 3,534 tons, Cunard
Built by William Hamilton at Port Glasgow, she was sold in 1965 to become the Greek-owned *Dimitris N.* In 1974 she became the Chinese-owned but Panamanian-registered *Asia Developer* and the *Fung Chi* in 1975. While under repair at Kaohsiung in 1975 she flooded and capsized. Salvaged, she was broken up in July 1976.

Media, 1963, 5,586 tons, Cunard
Built by Redhead, South Shields, she was sold in 1971 to the Western Australian Shipping Commission to become the *Beroona*. Later in 1978 she became the *Palm Trader* under Greek ownership. In 1987 she caught fire at Bandar Abbas in Iran and capsized and sank near Larak Island in the Persian Gulf.

As part of a bit of schoolboy physics practical I went on board and the duty officer kindly explained and demonstrated the use of a sextant to me.

East Asiatic Company (Det Ostasiatiske Kompagni A/S) Denmark

The Danish East Asiatic Company was founded by Hans Niels Andersen in Copenhagen in 1897. The initial objective was for passenger and freight services between Denmark, Thailand, what was then the Malay States, the Straits Settlements and the Far East. Eventually the route network embraced the Indian sub-continent, Indonesia, Australia and New Zealand and also the Caribbean and the west coast of North America.

The company was at the forefront in the development and operation of large motor ships with the pioneering *Selandia* being delivered from Burmeister & Wain amid much royal pomp and publicity in 1912. In an era when the number of funnels was an indication of power, the *Selandia* and many of her contemporaries were built without conventional funnels.

The company still exists, retaining considerable interests in Thailand, but as a widely diversified conglomerate.

Sinaloa, 1956, 8,812 tons
One of the final pair of eight S-class ships constructed between 1953 and 1956 for East Asiatic, the *Sinaloa* was built in Denmark at the Naksov yard. To enable her to be used on the Pacific services, in 1968 she was modified to carry more refrigerated cargo and her No. 2 hold was adapted for containers.

Sold in 1978 to Chinese interests to become the *Yuen Chau,* she was broken up in Bangkok in 1983.

Siena, 1954, 8,854 tons
Another of the eight S-class freighters built in Nakskov, Denmark, for the company as part of its major rebuilding programme. Sold in 1975 to become the Nigerian *D J Fajemirokum*, she sank off Casablanca while en route to Chittagong in December 1979.

Panama, 1950, 9,013 tons
Built at Kobe in Japan, she was the first of the five P-class ships that formed part of the seventeen-ship building programme. In 1972 she was sold to Chinese interests to become the *Celebes Sea* (Somali flag). She was transferred to the Chinese flag as the *Hong Qi 102* in 1975 and was eventually broken up as the last survivor of her class in 1983.

Elder Dempster Line

Elder Dempster Line was originally founded in 1868 to trade from Glasgow and chiefly Liverpool to West Africa. In 1909 control passed to Sir Owen Philips. After the collapse of the Royal Mail group, the company came under the management control of Alfred Holt's Blue Funnel Line. In 1957, when Nigerian National Line was established, the company took a 33 per cent share, selling out to the Nigerian government in 1961. In 1965 Elder Dempster Line came under the complete control of Blue Funnel.

The shipping company ceased when sold out to the French Delmas-Vieljeux. The shipping agency was wound up in 2000.

Obuasi, 1952, 5,895 tons
One of the five O-class ships built by Harland & Wolff, she was a cadet ship for Elder Dempster. She also operated as a 'pool' ship, likely to be routed anywhere where she was needed. She was sold to Hong Kong and renamed *Amoy*, flying the Somali flag. In August 1972, while en route from Penang to Calcutta, she stranded near Cape Negrais on the extreme south-west coast of Burma and west of the mouths of the Irrawaddy River, becoming a constructive total loss.

Above: *Eboe*, 1952, 9,380 tons

This has to be one of my best shots, as she gently moves away from the quay, catching the evening sunshine. A relatively large and fast (16 knots) motor vessel, she was built by Scotts of Greenock originally for the North America – West Africa run. She later operated from Europe to West Africa. She was sold in 1977 to Maldives Shipping of Panama to become the *Georgios* and later the *Georgia*. She was broken up in Kaohsiung in February 1978.

Opposite above: *Oti*, 1955, 5,485 tons

Another Harland & Wolff build for Elder Dempster. Unlike the earlier ships of the O class she was not fitted out to carry passengers and had a smaller superstructure. In 1968 she was involved in the rescue of some 120 people from Sapele at the start of the Biafran war. She was sold to Cypriot interests in 1972 to become the *Nicholas K* and was eventually scrapped in 1979.

Opposite below: *Degema*, 1959, 8,153 tons

Built by William Gray, West Hartlepool, she was named for a town in the River States of Nigeria. In 1979 she was sold to Honduras and renamed *Veejumbo*. She reverted to *Degema* in 1982 and arrived for scrapping at Gadani Beach in January 1983.

Perang, 1954, 6,177 tons
Built by William Gray in West Hartlepool and sold in 1972 to become the *Agnic* under the Greek flag, she was scrapped at Gadani Beach in May 1978.

Kaduna, 1959, 5,599 tons
Kaduna was originally built by Lithgows of Port Glasgow for the Glasgow-based Henderson Line. Although Henderson Line traded principally to the Far East and Burma (Myanmar) in particular, she was given the name of a town in Nigeria. She was briefly transferred to the Blue Funnel Group in 1972 before being sold in 1973 to Liberia to become the *Regent Reliance*, flying the flag of Singapore. She was re-registered under the Panamanian flag in 1975 and was broken up at Gadani Beach in 1978.

Ellerman Line

The Ellerman Line had been founded during the nineteenth century and expanded largely by acquisition to become one of the largest shipping companies in the world, trading globally. The 1967 edition of *Ocean Ships* describes the routes covered as world-wide and too numerous to give in detail. The mid-1950s fleet consisted of ninety-four ships and even in the early 1960s there were still fifty-nine, all having been built post-war. The company disappeared in the plethora of mergers and takeovers post-1970.

City of Chelmsford (ex-*Sambrake*, ex-*Lionel Copley*), 1943, 7,176 tons
In the late 1950s, the local bus company who also operated an impressive fleet of luxury coaches ran a summer evening town tour. This tour included the docks and on the evening I went on the trip, we saw the *City of Chelmsford* setting sail out of the docks and towards the open sea. I felt it would be invidious to omit such a memory.

Built by Bethlehem Fairfield as the *Lionel Copley*, she was completed as the *Sambrake* for the Ministry of War Transport under the Lease-Lend programme. Not returned to the US after the war, she was sold to Ellerman Lines in 1947. In 1960 she was sold and after a major refit, which included installing oil engines at nearby Newport (Mon.), she became the Panamanian *San George,* but flying initially the Greek flag. In 1961 she transferred to flying the Lebanese flag. In 1968 she was sold again to Cypriot buyers to become the *Suerte* and was broken up at Split in 1971. (Photographer Dave Leonard, Shipspotting.com)

Above: *Egyptian*, 1952, 3,512 tons
One of the Ellerman liners not named for a city. Built by J. L. Thompson & Son at North Sands, she briefly became the *City of Leicester* in 1964 before being sold to Greece to become the *Gardenia*. She was sold again in 1967 to Chinese interests to become the Panamanian-flagged *Chung Hsuing* and was broken up at Kaohsiung the same year.

Opposite above: *City of Swansea*, 1946, 9,959 tons
She was built by Barclay Curle at Whiteinch and sold to Ben Line in 1968 to become the *Benkitlan* and was broken up at Kaohsiung in 1972.
    Ellerman Line frequently honoured towns that had not achieved or been granted city status. The arrival of the *City of Swansea* in, I think 1962, prompted a front page picture in the local *Evening Post* newspaper.
    Ellerman Lines frequently put the namesake's coat of arms on the bow as a substitute figurehead. However, in this case it is absent.
    For the record, the town of Swansea was eventually granted city status in 1969 following the investiture of Prince Charles as Prince of Wales. (Photo by W. Moore, World Ship Society)

Opposite below: *City of Karachi*, 1951, 7,320 tons
Built by Denny's of Dumbarton, she was sold in 1972 to Greek owners to become the *Kavo Kolones*. In January 1974 she was broken up at Kaohsiung.

Ionian, 1947, 3,507 tons
Built by J. L. Thompson & Sons at North Sands, she became the *City of Durham* in 1964. She was sold the same year to Greek buyers to become *Angelica N* and again in 1968 to become the *Eliza*. She was broken up in Hamburg in 1971.

Patrician, 1947, 3,604 tons
An action shot of an early morning arrival in Swansea. She was built by J. L. Thompson at North Sands. Not long after this photograph was taken the ship was in collision with the American Grace liner *Santa Emilia* while en route from Constantia to Dublin and sank some 4 miles off Tarifa in Spain.

Federal/NZ

Federal Line traced its origins back to 1895. From 1904 it operated a joint service with Houlder Bros. to Australia and New Zealand. It was taken over by New Zealand Line in 1916 but continued to trade as a separate concern. The same year, New Zealand Line became part of the P&O empire. Federal Line named its ships for English counties.

New Zealand Line was founded by local farmers and traders in Christchurch (NZ) in 1873. Historically, their ships could be identified by their very pale buff funnels. In the 1960s this was replace by the Federal red and black with the house flag motive. New Zealand Line ships carried Maori names.

Papanui, 1943, 10,000 tons
Completed in Glasgow in 1943 by Alexander Stephen, she was one of five ships built under a commercial contract to replace war losses.

Unlike her sisters, she was not transferred to Federal Line, so she retained her pale buff funnel until the end of her days. She was sold in 1965 for breaking up in Kaohsiung.

A difficult shot with space limitations and I only possessed a Box Brownie.

Cumberland, 1948, 11,281 tons
One of eight ships built as part of the post-war replacement programme, five of which, including the *Cumberland*, were built at John Brown's Clydebank yard. She is seen berthed on the south side of the King's Dock, which indicates she is under repair or waiting to be dry docked for repairs. The *Cumberland* survived to be transferred to P&O in 1973 and get repainted in the new P&O blue livery with P&O in white on a light blue funnel. She was eventually scrapped in the Far East in 1976.

Surrey, 1952, 8,227 tons
Built by Alexander Stephens in Glasgow, she was transferred within the P&O Group in 1967 to British India Line and renamed *Juwara*. She was sold for scrapping in Taiwan in 1972.
  The noticeable feature about this ship was that she was smaller than the regular Federal and NZ liners that called into Swansea. Most were usually over 10,000 gross tons.

Cornwall, 1952, 7,583 tons
Another slightly smaller member of the fleet also built by Alexander Stephens in Glasgow and also transferred to British India Line in 1967 and renamed *Juna*. She was broken up in Kaohsiung in 1972.

Hertford, 1948, 11,276 tons
One of eight large refrigerated ships built as part of the post-war reconstruction programme. She survived long enough to transfer into the P&O General Cargo Division and even acquire the new P&O corporate blue. Unlike her sisters, she was sold for further trading becoming the Greek-Cypriot *Thia Despina* in 1976 but after grounding at Port Said in July 1977 she was declared a constructive total loss and laid up at Piraeus. However, she was purchased by other Cypriot interests in 1978, becoming the *Georghios Frangakis,* and was eventually scrapped at Aliaga in 1985.

This picture shows her berthed adjacent to the Queen's Dock, possibly waiting to be dry docked for repairs and overhaul.

Ardent purists may wish to correctly point out that Hertford is a shire and not a county!

The Furness Group

The Furness Group owed its origins to the original Furness Withy amalgamation in 1891. Furness Withy grew by acquisition and acquired the Prince Line in 1916. Royal Mail Lines was acquired in 1965 and Manchester Liners in 1970.

In 1969 the company joined with British and Commonwealth, P&O and Alfred Holt's Ocean Steamship to establish Overseas Containers Limited to exploit the move towards containerisation. That company became part of Orient Overseas Containers in 1980 and the Oetker Group in 1991.

Pacific Steam Navigation was formed in 1838 to operate from the UK to the west coast of South America. It was a pioneer in the use of steamships in the Pacific Ocean. Royal Mail bought Pacific SN in 1910, although it retained its separate identity. Following the takeover by Furness Withy in 1965, the Pacific SN ceased to be a separate entity. This diverse group is represented by ships from different group companies.

Houlder Brothers was formed in London in 1856. Originally operating with chartered tonnage, their first ship was acquired in 1861 and was used on the North Atlantic.

Later the company expanded with services to Australia, New Zealand and the Pacific Islands. Many of the ships, such as the *Thorpe Grange*, carried names suffixed by 'Grange'.

A Houlder Bros/Furness Withy joint venture with operating to Argentina was established in 1914.

Above: *Sarmiento*, 1943, 8,436 tons, Pacific SN
One of two sisters built by Harland & Wolff, she was sold to Greek interests in 1969 to become the *Monomachos* and sold again to Cypriot interests to become the *Gladiator*. She made her last voyage from Havana to Shanghai where she was broken up in 1971.

Royal Mail/Pacific having been taken over by the Furness Group means that she sports the Furness funnel colours.

Opposite above: *Manchester Trader*, 1955, 7,916 tons, Manchester Liners
A rare visitor to Swansea. Manchester Liners were part of the Furness Withy Group and had similar funnel colours. Built by Harland & Wolff at their Govan yard, she had previously done a long-term charter to Shaw Savill as the *Zealandic*. At the time she was on charter to Manchester Liners from another Furness Group member – the Prince Line. That might explain the rather unusual polished wooden name plate with gold lettering instead of the more usual painting or embossing of the name onto the hull.

Returned to Prince Line in 1969, she reverted to her original name of *Western Prince*. She was sold in 1971 to Cypriot interests and was renamed *Mariner* and was lost in March 1973, east of Japan, while en route from Havana to Kobe.

Opposite below: *Oakmore* (ex-*Empire Kent*, ex-*Levante*), 1939, 4,700 tons, Johnson Warren Line
Another part of the Furness Group, the *Oakmore* was originally built by Nordseewerke in Emden as the *Levante* for Deutsche Levant Line. She was captured in May 1945 at Oslo and given the name *Empire Kent*. Not all Empire-named ships were war standards. The Ministry of War Transport allocated Empire names to captured and confiscated enemy tonnage. She was sold to Johnson Warren Line in 1947 to become the *Oakmore* and was scrapped in 1967 at Aviles in Spain.

Another photograph taken during the prolonged winter of early 1963, taken using a Box Brownie with Kodak 620 film.

Above: *Westbury,* 1960, 8,533 tons, Houlder Bros (Alexander Shipping)
Houlder Bros operated through a variety of subsidiaries united by the distinctive black and red
funnel with a white Maltese cross. The *Westbury* was a modern tramp steamer transferred to Shaw
Savill without a change of name in 1975, was sold to Greece in 1978 to become the *Diamando,* and
became the *Polana* in 1980.

Opposite above: *Ocean Transport,* 1962, 8,608 tons, Houlder Bros
Some shipping companies only had one port of registry; historically, Blue Funnel and Cunard
ships were always registered in Liverpool. London and Southampton were also popular. However,
Houlder Bros were not so rigid and in 1962 the *Ocean Transport* was registered in Swansea. It was
a source of civic pride and there was a front page picture depicting the stern of the vessel and the
port of registry. She was probably one of the largest ships ever to be registered in Swansea. The ship
was sold in 1979 to become the Liberian *Ellion Hope.*
  I missed the opportunity to photograph this ship on her famous visit. She is depicted in the Royal
Victoria Docks, London. However, it would have been invidious to omit her.

Opposite below: *Thorpe Grange,* 1954, 8,695 tons, Houlder Bros
Another action shot as the ship is being nudged away from her berth towards the dock's exit. Built
by Bartrams at Wallsend, she became the *St Merriel* in 1966, reverting briefly and temporarily
to her original name in 1971. As the *St Merriel* she was sold to Singapore interests in 1973 and
eventually became the Malaysian-flagged *Liva*. While under arrest in Colombo in February 1978,
she broke her moorings and became involved in a collision. She was sold and renamed *Selemat
Sindin,* before being sold on to be broken up in Kaohsiung in 1977.

Guinea Gulf Line

Guinea Gulf Line owed its origins to an enterprising young man called John Holt from Liverpool, who sailed to Equatorial Guinea to work in a grocery store in 1862. In 1867 he bought out his employer and, in 1868, he acquired a schooner with his brother and opened up more trading posts in West Africa. Offices were opened in Liverpool in 1874, and the business entered the palm oil trade in 1881, expanding trade into Nigeria in 1887. The Guinea Gulf Line came into being in 1954.

Post-1962, political and economic unrest in both Ghana and Nigeria made trading conditions difficult. There was also competition from the countries' own emerging shipping companies. The company management was taken over by Brocklebank Line in 1963 until its sale to Elder Dempster Line in 1965, who replaced the Guinea Gulf ships with their own tonnage.

Elizabeth Holt, 1953, 5,580 tons The *Elizabeth Holt* was built by Cammel Laird at Birkenhead and was sold to Greece in 1965. After several owners and changes of name, she was scrapped at Kaohsiung in 1973.

Florence Holt, 1953, 5,581 tons Also built by Cammel Laird, she too was sold in 1965. After several changes of ownership and name, she was scrapped at Kaohsiung in 1974.

Harrison Line

The Harrison Line (officially T. & J. Harrison) was founded by two brothers in Liverpool in 1853. Initially it traded by importing brandy from the Charente area of France. Later it expanded activities to Iberia, then India and East Africa and eventually the West Indies and Central America. The company ceased trading in 2000.

Harrison Line named their ships for trades and professions, although this was widely interpreted.

Film buffs will recognise that it was the wreck of a Harrison Line ship that was the background to the famous film *Whisky Galore!*

Herdsman, 1947, 6,822 tons
This photograph must have been taken at the end of this ship's time with Harrison Line. She was sold to Hong Kong buyers in 1965.

Administrator, 1958, 8,714 tons
Sold to Stena Atlantic Line and renamed *Tyne*, she was then sold on to Singapore to become the *Oriental Sea*.

Barrister, 1954, 8,366 tons
Built by Doxfords, she was one of four sisters that in turn were part of a larger group of ten ships. All were sold to Greek-Cypriot buyers in the early 1970s, the *Barrister* becoming the *Georgy*. The *Barrister* had the dubious distinction of being the last of the ten to be broken up at Castellon in 1984.

Lamport & Holt Line

Lamport & Holt Line was founded in 1845 as a partnership in Liverpool. George Holt was actually the brother of Alfred Holt of Blue Funnel Line fame. George Holt had also served an apprenticeship with another famous Liverpool shipping firm, T. & J. Brocklebank. In the 1860s they established a regular service of steamers to Brazil and the River Plate. These early steamers established the precedent of naming ships for famous men of science, art, and letters. The company was a pioneer in 1869 in the carrying of coffee from Brazil to the Americas and later frozen meat from the River Plate in 1886. The company was closely related to the Blue Star Line and also the Booth Line.

The 1966 edition of Bert Moody's *Ocean Ships* actually names Swansea along with Liverpool as a principle home port for Lamport & Holt Line services to Brazil, Uruguay and Argentina.

Above: Rubens (ex-Crispin), 1951, 4,472 tons
I suspect that this was one of my first attempts at ship photography with my faithful Brownie, possibly as early as 1961. It was certainly one of my earliest successful attempts.

Built by Pickersgill in Sunderland for the Booth Line, she was transferred to Austasia Line as the *Mandowi*. She was returned to Booth Line as the *Dunstan* but chartered to Lamport & Holt Line as the *Rubens*. She was sold to Greece in 1973 to become the *Irini K* and was broken up in Turkey in 1974.

Below: Rossetti, 1956, 4,538 tons, Lamport & Holt
Built by Pickersgill in Sunderland, she sailed as the *Rossetti* until 1963 when she was chartered to Booth Line as the *Boniface*. She returned to Lamport & Holt in 1967, reverting to the name *Rossetti*. It was after this transfer that this picture was taken. In 1970 she was sold to Booth Line, reverting to the name *Boniface*, and was sold in 1974 to a Greek buyer to become the *Amaryllis*.

Opposite below: Dryden (ex-Columbia Star), 1939, 8,408 tons
Built by Burmeister & Wain in Copenhagen for the Blue Star Line as the *Columbia Star,* she was transferred to Lamport & Holt Line in 1953. She was transferred back to Blue Star in 1955 as the *Patagonia Star,* reverting to her original name in 1957. She returned to Lamport & Holt Line in 1963, a year before this picture was taken. It was one of my earliest 35 mm photographs with my newly acquired Voigtlender Vito C. She was eventually sold for breaking up in Kaohsiung in 1968.

Debrett, 1940, 8,104 tons
One of a series of seven ships built by Harland & Wolff that were readily recognisable because of
their very striking design of superstructure. The *Debrett*, the fifth of the series, had a wide funnel
containing the wireless room, which extended to the front of the bridge. She served briefly as the
Blue Star *Washington Star* in 1955 and was scrapped at Osaka in 1965.

Raeburn (ex-*Wanstead*), 1949, 9,010 tons (Watts Watts)
This ship had quite a colourful career. Built originally for the London-based Watts Watts Line as the
Wanstead, in 1957 she was chartered to Port Line as the *Port Wanstead*. Returned to Watts Watts
in 1960, she was chartered to Lamport & Holt Line in 1963, becoming the *Raeburn*. She returned
again to Watts Watts in 1964, becoming the *Wanlui,* before being sold in 1974 to become the
Maldive Explorer. She was eventually broken up at Gadani Beach in 1978.
    This was a fortuitous shot, catching the ship in a very brief window of an adventurous life.

Rossetti, 1950, 5,664 tons, (Watts Watts)
This was an evening shot with the last vestiges of sunlight catching the still water of the King's Dock. This ship was built in 1950 for Watts Watts Line as the *Woodford*. She was briefly chartered to Lamport & Holt Line as the *Rossetti* in 1963–64, when this photograph was taken. She was returned to Watts Watts in 1964 and was sold to become the *Woosung*. She was sold again in 1976 to become the *New Dragon* and was eventually broken up at Shanghai in 1978. Again, another lucky window.

J. Lauritzen, Denmark

Lauritzen Line (J. Lauritzen) was established as a timber trading company in Esbjerg in 1884. The first steamship was purchased in 1888 and the shipping company was established in 1895. It was a pioneer in the reefer trades, initially bringing fruit from Spain to England in 1905. This traffic was extended with similar traffic from Chile to New York in 1934.

The association with polar exploration dates from the delivery of the *Kista Dan* in 1953. After a maiden voyage to Greenland she was chartered to the Australian National Antarctic Expedition to enable the building of a permanent Australian base in Antarctica. The familiar and very distinctive red hulls date from 1955 when the *Kista Dan* was painted red to make her more visible in polar waters. The red hulls now symbolise the Lauritzen line.

The company and its ships are still in existence, albeit in a somewhat different format.

Helga Dan, 1957, 4,040 tons

It is a shame that these photographs are not in colour so we could appreciate the bright red hulls sported by Lauritzen ships. Built by Steulcken in Hamburg and equipped with an ice-strengthened maierform bow, she was famous for her battles with the winter ice along the St Lawrence River in Canada. In January 1964 she was the first ship of the new season to reach Montreal.

She was sold to Cypriot interests in 1974, becoming the *Mitsa K*, and switching to the Greek flag in 1976. In 1982 she was stranded at Hamsi Bay on the Bosphorus and, although re-floated, the damage was so severe that she was regarded as a constructive total loss and was towed to Greece for scrapping.

Varla Dan, 1960, 2,354 tons

Built at Arendal in Norway, she was sold to Finnish buyers in 1970 to become the *Warl* and was sold again in 1972 to Karlsen Shipping of Halifax, Nova Scotia, and renamed *Minna*. In August 1974, while engaged in oceanographic work under charter to the Bedford Institute of Oceanography, she ran aground in Brewer Bay, on the uninhabited Resolution Island (south-east of Baffin Island in the Hudson Channel), and became a total wreck in a storm the following October.

Saima Dan, 1962, 3,065 tons
Built at Gorinchem in the Netherlands, she was sold to Greece in 1975 to become the *Kostas K*. Laid up at Piraeus in 1983, she was eventually broken up at Eleusis, north-west of Piraeus, in early 1986.

Thora Dan, 1956, 4,041 tons
Also built by Steulcken in Hamburg and equipped with an ice-strengthening mierform bow, she was sold to Cypriot interests to become the *Elias K*.

Lykes Line

Lykes Line traces its origins back to the American Civil War when Dr Howell T. Lykes started collecting and delivering cattle to the Confederate soldiers in Florida. Later, cattle and fruit were being shipped to Cuba. The company came into being in 1898 and ships were named for family members. Originally specialising in trade between the US Gulf Coast ports, the Caribbean and South America, expansion into Europe, the Far East and the Mediterranean began in the 1920s. In 1954 it has the distinction of being the largest US cargo fleet still in private ownership. Shares were first offered to the public in 1958. In 1997 Lykes Lines became part of CP Ships and, following a further takeover by the German TUI Group, the brand name disappeared in 2005.

Eugene Lykes (ex-*Ocean Express*) 1945, 8,191 tons
Shipments of MG motor cars to the southern United States in 1963 brought a series of visits by Lykes Line ships.

The *Eugene Lykes* was an example of the C2-type standard cargo ship developed for the US Maritime Commission (USMC) as part of a major programme to completely rebuild the US merchant fleet. She was one of sixty-four modified type C2-S-AJ1 ships built by the North Carolina Shipbuilding Corporation. Launched as the *Ocean Express* but delivered as the *Eugene Lykes*, she was broken up at Kaohsiung in May 1970.

Ruth Lykes, 1945, 8,180 tons
A C2-S-AJ1 built by North Carolina Shipbuilding at Wilmington (NC) for the United States Marine Commission. Taken out of service in 1965 and laid up, she was eventually broken up in Kaohsiung in November 1971.

Stella Lykes, 1945, 8,180 tons
We have yet another C2-S-AJ1 from the shipyard in Wilmington (NC) for the USMC. Taken out of service in 1965 and laid up with the *Ruth Lykes*, she too was eventually scrapped in Kaohsiung in January 1971.

Above: *Shirley Lykes*, 1962, 9,889 tons

In 1960, Lykes Line started to take delivery of a new type of cargo vessel to replace their many aging C2s. They were distinctive-looking ships, with split superstructure and the conventional funnel replaced by two thin white (later black) parallel stacks that blended in with the kingposts. The company motif formerly on the funnel reappeared on the side of the forward superstructure. They were designated C3-S-37a.

The *Shirley Lykes* was built by Bethlehem Steel at Sparrows' Point (NJ) and was converted into a container ship in 1971, which increased her gross tonnage to 11,891. Retained as part of the National Defense Reserve Fleet, she was eventually scrapped at Chesapeake in 2005.

Opposite above: *Kendall Fish*, 1945, 8,230 tons

A C2-S-AJ1 standard cargo ship built by the North Carolina Shipbuilding Corporation at Wilmington (NC), originally for the US Maritime Commission. Purchased by Lykes Line in 1947, her only claim to fame was involvement in 1952 in a very protracted (ten years!) legal dispute over a damaged cargo of sisal being imported from North Africa into the United States. She was scrapped at Kaohsiung in December 1971.

Opposite below: *Frank Lykes* (ex-*Fairwind*), 1944, 8,168 tons

Yet another C2-S-AJ1 from the yard in Wilmington (NC). Purchased in 1947, she was scrapped at Kaohsiung in October 1970.

NASM (Holland America Line) The Netherlands

NASM was established in 1873 as the Netherlands' equivalent of Cunard. Like Cunard it operated a transatlantic passenger service. Never a Blue Riband contender and operating much smaller liners, it was still highly regarded. In addition to the passenger liners, there was a network of passenger cargo services to both the east and west coasts of North America.

It is interesting to note that some of the NASM promotional literature mentioned Swansea as a main UK calling point for the cargo liner services; doubtlessly this was because it was less of a diversion than Liverpool or Glasgow.

Now, like Cunard, only the cruising liners remain.

Dongedyk (ex-*Delftdyk*), 1929, 10,220 tons
She is described in the promotional literature of the day as a combi–liner, capable of carrying both cargo and a small number of passengers in accommodation that was of a very high standard. Originally built by Wilton-Fijenoord for the Europe–American West Coast run, she survived the war but was mined at the mouth of the Weser in 1950. She was repaired and extensively reconstructed with a new raked bow but retained her elegant counter stern, as well as gaining increased passenger accommodation and new engines that delivered a speed of 17 knots. Very much a victim of the container revolution and changing patterns of trade, she was broken up at Kaohsiung in 1966, not long after this photograph was taken.

Appingedyk (ex-*Coaldale Victory*), 1945, 7,624 tons
The Victory ships were an improved and faster (15 knots) version of the famous Liberty ships. Like the Liberty ships, the Victories were built using production-line methods. Laid down by Bethlehem/Fairfield at Baltimoe (MD) on 28 December 1944, the *Coaldale Victory* was launched on 23 February 1945 and completed and commissioned on 23 March, eighty-five days after her keel had been laid. She was named in honour of the outstanding production achievements of the Coaldale anthracite miners and their vital contribution to the war effort and national defence. She was even launched by a miner's daughter.

After a period laid up in the James River after the war, the ship was sold to Chinese interests, become the *Nanking Victory* in 1948, and in 1951 she became the Panamanian *Hassan*, and was eventually acquired by NASM in 1952. This photograph must have been one of my earliest as in 1962 she was sold again to become the Hong Kong *Mariner* and was eventually scrapped in Taiwan in 1972.

For a ship designed for a five-year life, twenty-seven years is not a bad achievement.

Palm Line

Palm Line was divested out of the United Africa Company in 1949. The company traded along the African coast from Morocco to Angola. To navigate the many creeks the ships had to be less than 500 feet long (in this case 460) and not draw more than 27 feet. To enter the Escravos River in Nigeria, a maximum of 17 feet was permitted over the bar.

The 1980s finally saw the end of Palm Line. A decline in traffic between Europe and West Africa resulted in Palm Line being sold in 1986.

Ilesha Palm, 1961, 5,682 tons
The *Ilesha Palm* was built by Swan Hunter. She was sold to the Greek Chaldeos Freighters and was registered in Liberia. Laid up at Mini Saqr in 1982, she was eventually towed to Karachi for scrapping in 1984.

Safmarine (South African Marine Corporation) South Africa

Safmarine owes its origin to a pioneering venture established in 1946 by South African industrialists and American ship-owners. Services began following the acquisition of three Victory ships. During the 1950s and 1960s there was a strong association with the UK-based British & Commonwealth shipping group. The company has grown to become a major north/south operator, noted for its African expertise. In 1999 the company became part of the Danish Maersk group but retains much of its individual identity. Safmarine containers can be readily observed on European roads and railways and the ships retain their grey hulls with Safmarine displays on the side.

South African Victory, 1945, 7,605 tons

This ship was a genuine pioneer. She started life as the *Westbrook Victory*, one of over 500 Victory-type standard cargo ships built in the United States towards the end of the Second World War. They were regarded as an improvement on the earlier Liberty ships. Laid up in the James River after the war, she was eventually one of three such ships bought in 1947 by the newly established South African Marine Corporation (Safmarine). She was named *Vergelegen*. In 1961 she acquired the ponderous appellation *South African Victory*, which was reduced to *S A Victory* in 1966. She was broken up in Taiwan in 1969.

South African Statesman (ex-*Bosbok*, ex-*Clan Sinclair*), 1950, 8,405 tons

Built by Greenock Dockyard for Clan Line as the *Clan Sinclair*, in late 1959 she was transferred to the Springbok Line as the *Bosbok*. She acquired her ponderous name when Springbok Line was acquired by Safmarine. This was later shortened to *S A Statesman* in 1966 and she ended her days at Kaohsiung in 1971.

Above: S A Vanguard (ex-*New Bern Victory*), 1945, 7,607 tons
The *S A Vanguard* (ex-*New Bern Victory*) was one of the first ships to be acquired in 1947, originally taking the name *Constantia*. From 1961 she acquired the ponderous name *South African Vanguard*, which was reduced to *S A Vanguard* in 1966. In remarkably good condition for her age and origin, the *S A Vanguard* loads her bottom cargo of tinplate.

The *New Bern Victory* was built in Bethlehem (NJ) in 1945. She was sold to Panamanian interests in 1969 and renamed *Isabena*. She was wrecked off the coast of Pakistan in July 1972.

Opposite above: South African Transporter (ex-*Simoa*), 1953, 9,603 tons
One of what Safmarine called the 'Global-class' ships. One of three ships built by Fairfields for Norwegian owners, acquired by Safmarine in 1958, in 1966 her named was reduced to the less ponderous *S A Transporter*. She was scrapped in 1972.

Opposite below: South African Trader (ex-*Sjoa*), 1954, 9,826 tons
Another Global-class ship built by Fairfields, originally for Norwegian owners. Acquired by Safmarine in 1958, she similarly had her name reduced in 1966 to *S A Trader*. Following a fire in 1972 she was broken up at Kaohsiung in the same year.

Safmarine ships or ships chartered to Safmarine were frequent visitors to load their bottom cargo of tinplate, which was vital to the South African economy at the time. A deal was done whereby the ships were turned round in forty-eight hours, irrespective of the day. As a result, weekend working was often required.

Above: *S A Shipper* (ex-*Umzinto* ex-*Clan Robertson*), 1954, 7,898 tons
This ship had a colourful corporate history. She was one of thirteen ships comprising the 'Clan Shaw' family built by Greenock Dockyard for Pacific SN and Clan Line, in this case as the *Clan Robertson*. In 1959 she was transferred to Bullard & King's Natal Line, becoming the *Umzinto*. When the new owners became the Springbok Shipping Company of Cape Town, she was renamed *Rooibok*. The company was taken over by Safmarine and she eventually became the *S A Shipper*. She was broken up at Kaohsiung in 1975.

Opposite above: *South African Seafarer* (ex-Clan Shaw), 1950, 8,101 tons
Because my bedroom overlooked the bay I could observe a ship passing Mumbles Head and collecting the pilot before jumping on my bicycle to meet the ship as she entered the docks. Still with her ponderous name, the *South African Seafarer* arrives in Swansea in late 1965. The obvious link with the Union Castle and Clan Line group is seen in the ship's profile. She had started life as the *Clan Shaw* in 1950. En route from Glasgow to Beira in the summer of 1966 she was wrecked on 1 July at the entrance to Cape Town harbour, fortunately without loss of life.

Opposite below: *S A Merchant*, 1955, 9,866 tons
Originally built by Fairfields of Govan for the Global Maritime Transport of Panama on behalf of Norwegian owners, she was acquired by Safmarine as one of the four Global-class ships without ever taking a Global name. She became a cadet training ship in 1966 and ended her days in the scrapyard at Kaohsiung in 1977.

Ove Skou Line, Denmark

The Skou Line was set up in Denmark 1935 and the ships were named for family members. After the Second World War the company expanded and by 1970 employed 800 sea-going staff. By 1974 it was Denmark's third largest shipping company with twenty-six ships. The company was sold to eventually become part of the Norwegian Tschudi Shipping Group, which is still active.

Above: *Benny Skou*, 1951, 4,248 tons
Built by Burmeister & Wain in Copenhagen, she was renamed *Else Skou* in 1966. She was sold to Greece to become the *Synergasia* in 1972 and was broken up in Burriana, Spain, in November 1979.

Opposite above and below: *Skou Neptun* (ex-*Jytte Skou*), 1949, 3,885 tons and *Jytte Skou*, 1949, 6,650 tons
Built by Burmeister & Wain in Copenhagen, she was renamed in 1964. In March 1966, while on passage from Callao to Arica in Chile with general cargo but also drummed chemicals, she ran aground in dense fog and was wrecked 20 miles south of San Juan in Peru.

Grete Skou, 1959, 4,211 tons
Built by Helsingor Skibsvaerft in Elsinore, she was sold in 1974 to become the *Master Tony K.* She was broken up at La Spezia in June 1984.

The appearance of so many of the Skou Line ships in 1962/63 was due to the need to ship large quantities of cars to the southern United States. The cars, mostly the legendary MG sports cars and the MG Sports Sedan, were brought down from Oxford and Abingdon and loaded onto the ships. Much to the great glee of the dock workers, they had to be driven from the warehouse to the loading point! The quayside was like Le Mans!

Mette Skou, 1963, 4,262 tons
Also built by Helsingor Skibsvaerft, she was sold in 1979 to become the *Melantho C,* flying the Greek flag. In 1982 she was transferred to Panamanian registry. In 1982 she was sold to Chinese interests but in 1988 she acquired the name *Lee* and flew the flag of St Vincent and the Grenadines. She was scrapped at Chittagong in February 1989.

Union Castle Line

The Union Castle Line was formed in 1900 by the merging of the rival Union Line, which dated from 1853, and Donald Currie's Castle Line, which had come into existence in 1872. The company operated the lucrative mail service from England to South Africa. The regular mail service was to continue into the 1960s. There was also a six-ship monthly intermediate round-Africa fleet that circumnavigated the African continent – three ships going in each direction. Each voyage took about two months. In addition there was a fleet of fast refrigerated ships – the 'R' class, bringing food products from South Africa. There was also a small fleet of cargo ships. The distinctive feature of all Union Castle Line ships, except the general cargo ships after 1954, was the lavender-grey hull colour.

In 1956 the company merged with Clan Line to form the British and Commonwealth Shipping Group and had a strong association with the South African Marine Corporation. Shipping operations ceased in 1977.

Rowallan Castle, 1943, 7,943 tons

Union Castle liners were unusual visitors. The British Commonwealth group was more usually represented by the Clan Line. The R-class refrigerated ships were built to carry fruit from South Africa to Europe. Despite the date, the *Rowallan Castle* was not built by Harland & Wolff for the Ministry of War Transport. Capable of 16 knots, she and her sisters were employed during the war to bring foodstuffs to Britain without escort. For a merchant ship she was heavily armed and equipped with anti-mine defences. After an uneventful peacetime career, she was broken up at Kaohsiung in September 1971.

Above: Rothesay Castle, 1960, 9,650 tons
A refrigerated ship, ostensibly the last of the Union Castle R class, but in appearance more akin to the contemporary Clan Line ships, she was the only R-class built at Greenock Dockyard, while all the others had been built by Harland & Wolff. She was sold in 1975 to Uruguay to become the *Laura*.

Opposite above: Roxburgh Castle, 1945, 7,996 tons
The third of three R-class sister ships built during the war by Harland & Wolff. She had an uneventful career, being broken up in Shanghai in July 1971.

Opposite below: Rustenberg Castle, 1946, 8,342 tons
One of two slightly larger R-class ships delivered by Harland & Wolff after the war, she was named for a small town in the Transvaal that is a centre for growing citrus fruit, tobacco and cotton. She was broken up in Shanghai in September 1971.

Tribute to the War Standards

The demands of the Second World War required ships to move the extra amounts of cargo and materials, and also for ships to be built quickly to replace those that were lost. The British Ministry of War Transport came up with a 10,000 dwt tramp steamer to fill the urgent need. These ships were built using standard components and many survived the war to continue into commercial service. These ships carried names prefixed by 'Empire' and are represented by the former *Empire Nerissa*.

Above: *Nicolaos Michalos III* (ex-*Hubert Howe Bancroft*), 1942, 7,500 tons, Greece
Built by the Californian Shipbuilding Corporation, she became the *Global Spinner* in 1947, the
Vinje in 1948 and the *Vinstra* in 1949 before becoming the Greek-owned *Nicolaos Michalos III*
in 1953. She was loading baled scrap for the Far East when this picture was taken and it is likely
that both ship and cargo were en route to the scrapyard. She was broken up at Whampoa, China,
in May 1967.

Opposite above: *Albur* (ex-*Willaim Peffer*), 1944, 7,500 tons, Uruguay
One of the legendary wartime Liberty ships built by the Permante Metals Corporation at their
Richmond (California) No. 2 yard, she became the French *Lisieux* in 1947, the *Bar de Luc* in 1952
and the Italian *Andrea Parodi* in 1954. After some modification she became the *Albur* in 1960,
initially flying the Liberian flag, but changing to the Uruguayan flag in 1962. After some abortive
scrap metal deals she was eventually broken up in Shanghai in January 1969, sailing out there
flying the Red Duster and registered in Brixham!

Opposite below: *Al Amin* (ex-*Student*, ex-*Samarinda*, ex-*Samson Occum*), 1943, 7,252 tons,
Lebanon
She was one of a large batch of Liberty ships built by the California Shipbuilding Corporation.
Launched as the *Samson Occum,* she was completed for the British Ministry of War Transport as
the *Samarinda*. In 1947 she was acquired by Harrison Line, becoming the *Student*. She was sold
in 1963 to become the *Parthenon* under the Liberian flag, before being sold again to Midsutra
Shipping Limited to become the *Al Amin*, flying the Lebanese flag. She became the *Fortune Sea*
under the Panamanian flag before being scrapped in Taiwan in 1967. She is captured loading coal
in the Prince of Wales Dock.

San Geatano (ex-*Samtrusty*), 1944, 7,227 tons, Cia de Nav 'Somerset' SA, Liberia
One of 385 Liberty ships built by Bethlehem-Fairfield Shipyard, she became one of the 200 loaned to the United Kingdom under Lease-Lend. Returned to the United States at the end of the war she became the Donaldson Line *Lakonia* in 1947, under a deal that allowed the United Kingdom to buy around ten of the Sam-class Liberty ships. She became the Liberian *Sangeatano* in 1960 and was broken up at Blyth in 1972.

    Coincidentally, she was scrapped at the same time as the *Santagata* (ex-*Goldstream Park*).

    The Sam ships had an unfortunate association with South Wales and the Bristol Channel. In April 1947, the *Samtampa* (ex-*Peleg Wadsworth*), en route in ballast from Middlesbrough to Newport, was wrecked and lost with all hands at Sker Point near Porthcawl. The Mumbles lifeboat, sent out to the wreck, was also lost with all hands.

Gaasterkerk (ex-*Reed Victory*), 1945, 7,637 tons, United Netherlands (VNSMNV), Netherlands
The Victory ship was a development of the earlier wartime Liberty ship. They were slightly larger and had more powerful engines. Some of the earlier design and welding problems encountered with the Liberties were also corrected. Laid down by the Oregon Shipbuilding Corporation at Portland, Oregon, on 20 February 1945, she was delivered on 29 April, a mere sixty-seven days later. Sold to VNSMNV in 1946, she was scrapped at Whampoa in 1970 after twenty-four years of service.

Santagata (ex-Goldstream Park), 1944, 7,130 tons, Panama

The Parks were Canada's equivalent to the American Liberty ships. They were built in Canadian yards and originally operated by the Park Steamship Company on behalf of the Canadian government. Built by the North Van Ship repairs yard in Vancouver (British Colombia), she was launched as the *Fort Harrison*. She became the *Cottrell* in 1946 and the *Santagata* in 1961 and was broken up at Blyth in January 1971. Here she is seen loading coal from one of the hoists in the King's Dock.

Kraljevica (ex-Empire Nerissa), 1943, 7,077 tons, Jugolinja, Yugoslavia.

Built by Harland & Wolff in Glasgow, she served two UK owners before being sold to Yugoslavia in 1959. An action shot, she is seen on a gloomy afternoon in late spring 1963 moving away from the quay in the King's Dock prior to going about in order to enter the lock that would enable her to gain access to the open sea. She ended her days at Split (Croatia) in 1966.

King's Dock Miscellany

Above: *Angarsles*, 1962, 4,562 tons, USSR
The need for timber for pit props meant that ships from the former Soviet Union were not uncommon. The Soviet timber ship *Angarsles* was built in Gdansk and was one of the eighty-five Volgoles-class freighters. She became the *North Sea* in 1986 and was broken up in 1988.

Opposite above: *Izhmales,* 1962, 2,872 tons, USSR
Information about some ships from behind the Iron Curtain was always difficult to obtain. This ship was renamed *Nikita* in 1993. Looking at my notes, I hope my transliteration of the name was accurate!

Opposite below: *Brooktor* (ex-*Willem Mennen*), 1954, 5,129 tons, Germany
Built by Nordseewerke in Emden in 1954, she became the *Brooktor* in 1959. She was sold in 1967 to become the Greek *Aristidis* and the *Athens Sun* in 1970. She was broken up in China in 1979.

Above: *Elgaren*, 1957, 8,124 tons, Rederi AB Transatlatic, Sweden
Built in Hamburg in 1975, she became the Saudi Arab *Al Hijaz*, and was scrapped at Gadani Beach in February 1983.

Opposite above: *Cape Howe*, 1962, 19,032 tons, Lyle Shipping
Even though Swansea could handle ships of up to 30,000 tons gross, this was a very large ship caught undergoing repair at the Palmer's Dry Dock. Built by Lithgows at Port Glasgow, she was sold in 1978 to become the Singapore-flagged *Al Tawwab* and was scrapped in China in 1984.

Opposite below: *Cardiff City*, 1962, 10,335 tons, Reardon Smith
This picture, taken from a vacant 'A' shed berth, shows a good view up the north side of the King's Dock. General cargo ships were also handled where the two ships shown are berthed, and there were also further general cargo facilities visible at the far end. As might be expected in a Welsh port, coal hoists, albeit idle, are also visible.

She was built by Wm Doxford in Sunderland and like a number of other contemporary ships her Doxford diesels initially gave bearing trouble. She was sold in 1972 to become the *Sara Lupu* but retained Reardon Smith management. She was sold again in 1980 to become the *Alpac Asia* and was eventually scrapped at Kaohsiung in 1986.

Above: *Mellum*, Germany
Ostensibly a Bristol City Line freighter, until close examination reveals she is another example of a ship under long-term charter to Bristol City Line.

Opposite above: *Disa*, 1953, 5,877 tons, Sweden
Built in Sweden, she became the *Vishamn* in 1971. This was the start of a number of transfers and name changes. The ship became the *Gabon Trader* in 1974, *Bianca* in 1979, *Pearl Valley* in 1980 and finally the *Vivacious*, flying the Honduras flag in 1981. She was scrapped at Kaohsiung the same year.

Opposite below: *Etha Rickmers*, 1959, 8,405 tons, Rickmers Linie, Germany
Built by Rickmers in Bremerhaven, this very smart, modern German cargo ship, well-equipped to handle heavy cargos, was sold to the China Ocean Shipping Company of Shanghai in 1964, not long after this photograph was taken. Renamed *You Hao,* she was broken up in Guangzhou in 1988.

Folke Bernardotte (ex-*Tronhjemsfjord*, ex-*Ringerd*), 1947, 3,941 tons, Prebensen & Blakstad, Norway
A standard 385-foot (117 meters) tramp steamer built by the Norwegian yard of Fredrikstad
Mekaniske Verksted as the *Ringerd*. In 1950 she became the *Trondhjemsfjord* of the prestigious
Norwegian America Line. She acquired the name *Folke Bernardotte* when she passed to Prebensen &
Blakstaad in 1955. In 1966, some eighteen months after this picture was taken, she was sold to
Italian buyers to become the *Spring*, under the Liberian flag. She was broken up at Split in 1971.

Gisela Vennmann, 1955, 2,067 tons, Germany
This ship had a bizarre history when it came to names and name changes. Built in Kiel, Germany,
as the *Burkhard Broham*, but briefly and temporarily renamed the *Don Roberto*, she eventually
became the *Gisela Vennmann* until 1965, a few months after this photograph was taken. Briefly
reverting to the name *Don Roberto*, she became the *Ever* until 1964. Another brief reversion followed,
this time to *Gisela Vennmann*, before becoming the *Seahorse* under the Panamanian flag. She ended
her days by capsizing in the Karnaphuli River near Chittagong in Bangladesh in November 1986.

Hereford Beacon, 1955, 6,913 tons, Phs van Ommeren (Medomsley S S)
Medomsley S S was the UK operation of the Dutch Phs van Ommeren NV. The *Hereford Beacon* was built by van der Giessen de Noord in Alblasserdam. In 1968 she reverted to Dutch ownership under the name *Scherpendrecht,* becoming the *Nike* in 1970 and the *Eastern Unity* under the Panamanian flag in 1975.

Kuciste (ex-*Annik*), 1,333 tons, Atlanksa Plovidba, Yugoslavia
I rarely photographed ships this small, but a Yugoslav-flagged ship was unusual. She is also unusually berthed between the Prince of Wales Dock and the King's Dock opposite 'A' shed.

   Completed in 1940 by Kaldnes Mekanska in Tonsberg, Norway, for Norwegian owners, she was sold to German owners in 1955 and to Yugoslavian owners in 1961, initially to Mediteranska Plovidba, acquiring the name *Kuciste* and being registered in Dubrovnik. She was sold in 1967 to Italian buyers, becoming the *Maestrale,* and was broken up at La Spezia in 1972.

Italian, 1963, 454 tons, Norway
Ostensibly a small Ellerman Line coaster but she is actually a Norwegian ship under charter. She was *Dita Smits* and was chartered to Ellerman Line from 1968 to 1971.

Bardu, 1962, Norway
Another load of steel coils brought this large (for the time) Norwegian bulk carrier into the King's Dock. She was broken up at Nantong in June 1985.

Jaladharati, 1957, 6,527 tons, Scindia SN, India
A long shot showing the King's Dock and the coal hoists. She was built in Lubeck by Lubecker Flender-Werke as one of six very attractive sisters. She was sold in 1980 to Tilani Shipping of Bombay to become the *Prabhu Parvati* and was broken up in Bombay in 1982.

Muristan, 1950, 8,408 tons, Srick Line (Shahristan Steamship Co.)
Part of Strick Line's post-war rebuilding programme, she was one of three sisters built by Redhead at South Shields. In 1966, as the only sister still in the Strick Line fleet, and not long after this picture was taken, she was sold to Greece to become the *Atlas Trader*, and was then sold on to become the Liberian *Yaling* in 1970, before being broken up in Kaohsiung in 1972.

Mayis, 1961, 3,652 tons, Turkey National, Turkey
Built in Japan, one of a series of sister ships, she may have been named for the coup d'état that took place in Turkey in 1960. The date is also significant in the establishing of public holidays in secular Turkey. She became the *Kapten Teknekuran* in 1987.

Mithat Pasa, 1961, 3,636 tons, Turkey National, Turkey
Built in Japan, she was scrapped in 1993.

Olau Gorm (ex-*Greta Dan*), 1952, 4,615 tons, Denmark
Originally built for the Lauritzen Line, she became the *Olau Gorm* in 1963. She was sold in 1970 to become the *Santa Eudocia* and went through two further name changes before becoming the *Fast Breeze* in 1976. Following stranding damage in July 1978, she was broken up at Gadani Beach in January 1979.

Above: *Salvina*, 1963, 8,872 tons, Christian Salvesen
The approximate date of this picture indicates that the ship was less than a year old when it was taken. She was built by Oskarshamn on the east coast of Sweden. In 1972 she became the *Dawn Grandeur*, in 1976 the *Despina R* and in 1979 the *Diaklis*. Laid up in Stylis in 1982, she was reactivated in late 1984 as the *Kodrington* and loaded from Sibenik for the Far East. She made her final voyage from Cebu to Shanghai for breaking up in March 1985.

Opposite above: *Patmos* (ex-*Andros Gale*), 1957, 9,975 tons, Liberia
Large but short-term flows often brought unusual and interesting ships into Swansea. In late 1963 and into 1964, substantial amounts of coiled steel were coming through. This was one such load discharging in the King's Dock one evening in September 1963.

The ship was built by Ishikawajima in Japan and became the *Patmos* in 1960. She was sold to become the *Fede* in 1966.

I recall thinking at the time that the name was familiar but to my shame I could not make the connection. Eschatology was never one of my strong subjects!

Opposite below: *World Jonquil*, 1959, 10,499 tons, Niarchos Group, Liberia
One of the famous Niarchos Group ships, although they are mostly associated with large tankers. She became the *Theresa* in 1965 and *Minlly* in 1969 and was broken up at Kaohsiung in 1977.

Above: *Ravenstein*, 1947, 8,036 tons, Nord Deutscher Lloyd (NDL), Germany
Originally laid down as *Regensburg* in the Belgian Cockerill yard in 1943, one of three sisters, she was confiscated on the slipway in 1944. Eventually launched and completed in 1947, she was allocated to Cie Maritime Belge as the *Bastogne* for their Antwerp–New York service. The three ships were unusual in having four masts, rather like Edwardian liners, and triple screws. They were capable of over 19 knots.

In 1955 NDL bought them back and she became the *Ravenstein,* operating on their Far Eastern services. She survived the merger with Hamburg Amerika Line (HAPAG) but in 1974 she was sold to Cypriot buyers and was eventually scrapped at Gadani Beach in 1978.

Opposite above: *Baron Oglivy,* 1956, 5,471 tons, Hogarth
Here we have another classic Welsh port picture of coal being loaded, this time in the King's Dock. Built by Redhead at South Shields and powered by a combination of steam reciprocating engines and a low pressure turbine, she was one of six tramp steamers built for Hogarth between 1954 and 1956. In 1963, not long after this photograph was taken, she was sold to become the Liberian *Romeo* and in 1967 became the Greek-registered *Aghia Anastasia*. In September 1969, leaking badly, she was abandoned in the Indian Ocean at 32S 75E while on passage from Port Pirie to the Bristol Channel with a cargo of metal ore.

Opposite below: *Silversea* (ex-*Totem Queen*, ex-*Norse Reef*), 1963, 12,227 tons, Silver Isle Navigation, Bermuda
Photographed, possibly towards evening, in the Palmers Dry Dock. She was quite a large ship for the time as it was unusual for ships in excess of 10,000 tons gross to appear. Since this could not be later than 1965, this was this ship's third name in almost as many years.

Built in France at La Seyne sur Mer, she was purchased from Fulcrum Shipping. In 1972 she was sold to Chinese interests becoming the *Coral Sea* and was registered in Somalia. She changed registry to Panama in 1976 and was scrapped in China in 1986.

Above: *Sunny Prince* (ex-*Tijuca*), 1926, 8,665 tons, Olaf Pedersen, Norway
Originally built by Chantiers et Ateliers de St Nazaire for Wilhelm Wilhemsen, Oslo, as the refrigerated cargo ship *Tijuca*, she had her refrigerated capacity removed in 1937. In January 1941 she was mined in the Bristol Channel while en route from Avonmouth to Barry. She was towed into Barry, repaired, and returned to service.

She became the *Sunny Prince* in 1952 and was sold to the Chinese in 1968 to become the *Hoping 48* and was scrapped in 1976.

She probably has the distinction of being the oldest ship I photographed in Swansea.

Opposite above: *Iraouaddy*, 1953, 6,929 tons, Messageries Maritimes, France
Cie Messageries Maritimes was the French equivalent of P&O, trading from northern Europe and Marseille to East Africa and the Far East.

This was an unusual visitor in the early autumn of 1963. Having just passed 'O' Level French with oral proficiency, I went on board to get some practice!

Built by Forgieres et Chantiers de la Mediterranee at La Seyne for the Dunkerque–Australia route, after a somewhat uneventful life she was scrapped in 1973.

Opposite below: *Stove Waggon*, 1957, 9,898 tons, Norway
The *Stove Waggon* was built by Burmeister & Wain as the Swedish *Bellina*. In 1963 she became the Norwegian *Stove Waggon*. She retained Norwegian identity when she became the *Ranella* in 1965. In 1974 she was sold to Somali interests to become the *Ljuta,* later switching to Maltese ownership without a change of name. In 1980 she became the Panamanian *Sabik* before reverting to her original name in 1981, probably for her final voyage to Gadani Beach for breaking up.

Above: *Oranyan* (ex-La *Hacienda*), 1953, 6,009 tons, Nigerian National Line, Nigeria
Built in Newcastle for the London-based Buries Markes Line, she was sold to Nigerian National
Line in 1960. Nigerian National Lines had been established a year earlier as part of the drive
to get emerging nations to run their own merchant fleets. Even so, it was one-third owned by
Elder Dempster Line and 16 per cent by Palm Line. The majority shareholder was the Nigerian
government. In 1976 the *Oranyan* was sold to Greece to become the *Mathios Apessanikis* and
later became the *Marilaki*, still under the Greek flag, in 1978. She was broken up at Kaohsiung
in August 1980.

Nigerian National Line was never a long-term success, going into serious decline in the late 1980s
and was eventually wound up in 1995.

This photograph was a landmark in November 1964. It was the last shot with the old Brownie.
From then on, the 35 mm Voigtlender held sway!

Opposite above and below: *Mofjell*, 1946, Norway
Launched in 1941, she was completed as the tanker *America* by Deutsche Werft in Hamburg in
1946. She became the *Mofjell* in 1958 and in 1960 was converted to become an ore carrier. In 1965,
not long after this photograph was taken, she became the *Seven Suns*, later becoming the *Bulk
Transport* in 1967, and was eventually broken up at Gadani Beach in 1969.

Above: *Kollbris*, 1960, 12,808 tons, Norway
An arrival, this time locking in. This picture ticks two boxes – almost an action shot, but also restrictions on access to the Queen's Dock where the tankers unloaded, which meant that it was never easy to photograph oil tankers. Little else is known about this ship, but the name was certainly continued in a successor in 1975.

Opposite above: *Prosper* (ex-*Anna Odland*), 1939, 5,050 tons, Soldstatds Rederi, Norway
This ship is unusual because of her maierform bow. She was built by Bremer Vulkan in Germany as the *Anna Odland* for Jacob Odland. She served with distinction in the Second World War, sailing in both convoys and, despite a speed of only 13 knots, frequently alone. She became the *Prosper* in 1960 and at the time of the photograph was under charter to Ellerman Lines. In 1964 she became the *Soldrott*, still flying the Norwegian flag, but was sold to Cypriot interests in 1971. She was sold on to further Cypriot interests in 1975 and was eventually scrapped after forty years' service in 1979 at Gadani Beach.

Opposite below: *Norholt*, 1961, 5,723 tons, Ivaran Lines, Norway
Bristol City Line ships were regular visitors. A number of their ships were on long-term charter. The *Norholt* was built at Nakskov in Denmark and was on long-term charter to Bristol City Line for five years. At the end of the charter in 1966, she was renamed *Salvador*. Sold to Greece in 1977 to become the *San Juan*, she was wrecked en route to Jeddah in January 1982. Towed to Suez Bay and beached, she was later burnt out and beached on the Sinai side of the bay. It is not clear if the wreck was subsequently broken up.

Havgast, 1963, 11,504 tons, A/S Havkong, Norway
This ship is noticeable because of the large piece of self-discharging equipment on her deck. She was built in Germany and eventually sold to Greek buyers in 1974. She was sold on again to Far Eastern buyers in 1979 and was eventually scrapped in China in 1995.

Irish Plane, 1963, 10,449 tons, Irish Shipping, Eire
Another large shipment of steel coils brought this unusual visitor into Swansea in the early spring of 1964. Built in the Netherlands by Verolme, she spent much of her later life with Irish Shipping, conveying phosphates from North Africa. She became the *Salamis* in 1976 and the *Ionian Wave* in 1985. She was broken up at Gadani Beach in January 1986.

Tolmi (ex-*Biographer*), 1949, 6,791 tons, Liberia
Built for the Harrison Line in 1949, she had been recently (1964) sold to become the Liberian-registered *Tolmi*. She was broken up in Kaohsiung in January 1971.

Popi P K, 1937, 4,896 tons, Katsoulakos, Greece
Built originally in 1937 by Gotaverken in Gothenburg as the *Goonawarra* for Swedish owners, she was sold to Swedish buyers in 1956 to become the *Dakota* and again in 1962, becoming the *Salome*, although still under the Swedish flag and ownership. In 1965 she was sold to Katsoulakos to become the *Popi P K*.

In late December 1968, while en route from the Amazon River to Leixos in Portugal with a cargo of logs, she suffered a major engine room fire. While under tow and attempting make Las Palmas, she sank.

Above: *Sunfalcon*, 1944, 5,889 tons, Saguenay Terminals (Charter), Norway
A C1-class American standard freighter built at Beaumont (PA). The C1 class was part of a programme set up under the United States Marine Act of 1936 whereby the US merchant fleet was to be completely rebuilt with modern fast freighters. The C1 was the smallest of the four classes (C1 – C4) and the flush-decked hull clearly seems to anticipate the wartime Liberty ship. The *Sunfalcon* was actually classified C1-B, readily recognized by her wrap-around bridge and short boat deck.

When photographed she was on a long-term charter to Saguenay Terminals. During her life the ship sailed under a variety of names, having started life as the *Cape Faro*, becoming the *Crux* in 1954, *Grey Master* in 1960 and the *Siredal* in 1963. In 1968 she briefly became the *Concordia Falcon* and then *Sol Tulla*, but it was as the *Scandia Falcon* she arrived at Kaohsiung for breaking up in January 1973.

Opposite above: *Rio Cuarto*, 1950, 6,029 tons, ELMA, Argentina
Built by Monfalcone in Italy for the newly established Argentine merchant marine, she remained in service until broken up in La Plata in 1982.

Opposite below: *Sunvard*, 1957, 8,935 tons, Saguenay, Norway
Saguenay was a Canadian shipping company. Much of its ocean-going tonnage was on long-term charter or flew foreign flags. Built by Kockums of Malmo, the *Sunvard* was an unusual visitor. She became the *Sunleaf* in 1966, then the *Marianne* in 1970, before finishing her days as the *Kalikan*, flying the Honduran flag.

Above: *Vologdales*, 1962, 2,778 tons, USSR
This fine modern-looking ship became the Maltese-flagged *Patriot* in 1992. Several subsequent changes of name followed until she became the *Amir A* in 2000. Reports on the ship-spotting website are conflicting, but she might be still active.

Opposite above: *Tourcoing*, 1947, 6,780 tons, Wilhelm Wilhelmsen, Norway
Built by Kockums of Malmo, Sweden, she was sold in 1967 to the Panamanian Cia Nav. Marnuestro, but was managed by Karageorgis of Piraeus, taking the name *Tourcoing* and flying the Greek flag. She was broken up in Taiwan in 1973.

Opposite below: *Vlist*, 1956, 9,212 tons, Mij Houtvaart, Netherlands
Built in Hamburg, she was eventually sold to Cypriot buyers to become the *Enarxis*.

Queen's Dock

BP Tanker Company

BP Shipping is the oldest continually operating company in the vast multi-billion turnover BP Group. It started life as the BP Tanker Company in 1915 to carry the petroleum products of the then Anglo-Persian Oil Company.

The establishment of the UK's first crude oil refinery at nearby Llandarcy in 1922 was the beginning of regular BP tanker arrivals into Swansea's Queen's Dock.

British Resource, 1949, 11,200 tons
This was a rare opportunity to get a reasonable picture in the Queen's Dock. She was built by Hawthorn Leslie at Hebburn on the Tyne. She was slightly larger than the wartime standard T2 tanker and was broken up in Spain in April 1972, displaced by age and the fact that tankers were being built that were at least six times her size.

Above: *British Envoy*, 1953, 11,349 tons
Built by Doxfords at the Pallion Yard in Sunderland, she carried the name *Clyde Envoy* from 1958 to 1963 while operating for BP Clyde Tanker Co. After an uneventful career, she was broken up at Inverkeithing in April 1970.

Below: *British Mallard*, 1960, 11,174 tons
This rather long shot show the difference between being full and down and riding high when empty. The *British Mallard* has either just arrived with a cargo of crude for the local Llandarcy refinery, or has loaded petroleum products from the refinery and is ready to depart. She was built by Harland & Wolff in Belfast and was sold in 1978 to become the French-flagged *Penhors*. In 1984 she was sold again to Fal Bunkering under the Sharjah flag, taking first the name *Fal XII* then *Fame 2*, before being broken up at Gadani Beach in 1987.

British Holly, 1965, 13,270 tons
Built by Lithgows, Port Glasgow, she was quite new when this picture was taken. She was also quite a large tanker compared with the more traditional visitors and also sported the new trend in placing all the superstructure aft. She was sold in 1983 to Italian buyers and was then sold on again in 1990 to Turkish buyers to become first the *Emire* and then the *Para*. She was broken up in Aliaga in September 2006 after an impressive forty-one-year life.

British Sportsman, 1951, 11,231 tons, British Tanker Co. (later BP Tanker Co.)
Built by Swan Hunter at Wallsend, after an uneventful working life she was broken up by T. W. Ward
at Inverkeithing in January 1972.
   One of my first ship photographs – a rather long shot in the Queen's Dock in 1962.

Queen's Dock Miscellany

Forest Hill, 1961, 12,700 tons, Wm H. Muller, Netherlands
An action shot taken in the late spring of 1963. Built by Verolme in the Netherlands, she was sold in 1973 to become the *Five Valleys* under the Liberian flag. She was broken up at Gadani Beach in July 1983.

Ianthe, 1953, 12,333 tons, Liberia
Built at Haverton Hill as the *Merchant Baron* for what was known as the 'London Greek' (Lykiardopolou), she became the *Ianthe* in 1963. She became the *European River* in 1973, the *Theodorus V* in 1975 and the *Al-Dammam* later in the same year. She suffered a major fire near Agioi Theodoroi in June 1976 and was broken up in Barcelona in 1979.

Above: North Earl, 1956, 12,402 tons, Liberia
A rather pleasing action shot coming out of the Queen's Dock. She was originally built by Charles Connell as the *Scotstoun* and became the *North Earl* in 1962. She was broken up in Spain in 1977.

Opposite below: Hamilton Trader, 1959, 12,290 tons, Trader Line
Built by Blyth Dockyard and Shipbuilding. After a period laid up in the River Blackwater in 1973 she was sold to embark upon a career that involved many changes of name in fairly quick succession. It was as the *Georgios S* that she was eventually broken up at Chittagong, Bangladesh, in 1987.

Clearly empty and riding high, her position in the Queen's Dock suggest she is waiting to enter the dry dock for repairs.

Above: *Vivi,* 1957, 10,375 tons, Halfdan-Ditlev Simonsen, Norway
It was never easy to take photographs in the Queen's Dock. Entry was actually forbidden, so views such as this from a bank above the King's Dock were the best one could do. The *Vivi* was typical of the many chartered tankers that could be seen. She was eventually broken up in China in 1970.

Opposite above: *Lysefjell,* 1960, 13,327 tons, Olsen & Ugelstad, Norway
Originally launched in Fredrikstad as the *Bright Mountain,* she was delivered to Olsen & Ugelstad as the *Lysefjell.* She was converted to become a solvent tanker in 1969, which increased her deadweight tonnage from 20,000 to 21,032. She became the *Bjorgheim* in 1972 and the Panamanian-flagged *Maya Farber* in 1978. In 1983 she was sold again, retaining the Panamanian flag but becoming the *RAAD Al-bakry VIII.* She was reflagged under Saudi registry. In 1984, while en route from Ras Tanura to Jeddah, she was attacked by gunboats in the Persian Gulf, fortunately without serious casualties.

   In January 1990 an explosion in a cargo tank at Port Sudan led to a major fire. She broke in half and was declared a constructive total loss. The stern half sank but the bow was towed to Alang in India for breaking up.

Opposite above: *Marieborg,* 1956, 12,666 tons, Rederi AB Ragne, Sweden
Another chance to capture a charter tanker in the Queen's Dock. The *Marieborg* was built by Gotaverken in Gothenburg. She was sold to Finnish buyers in 1968, becoming the *Taifun,* and again in 1974 to French buyers to become the *Port Cros.* There then followed periods of being laid up, in both Gothenburg and Pireaus, before being eventually sold to Greek buyers and renamed *Salambo.* Another lay period followed and after another change of ownership and being renamed *Regal II* she was eventually broken up at Gadani Beach in July 1983.

Orlando, 1960, 14,123 tons, C. T. Bowring
The oil industry has always relied on a substantial amount of charter tonnage. This was an unusual opportunity to photograph one such tanker from the north side of the Queen's Dock. The *Orlando* was built by Lithgows on the Clyde. She was sold to Norwegian buyers in 1966 to become the *Stolt Falcon* and later became the *Stolt Pioneer.* After three further changes of ownership and two flags as the Greek-owned *Varkiza,* she was broken up at Kaohsiung in 1983.

Pepita, 1957, 12,369 tons, Hvalfangerselkapet, Norway
Built in Uddevalla, Sweden, she spent much of her operational life under charter to Shell.
In 1971 she suffered an engine breakdown near Christmas Island while en route to Australia. A Dutch tug towed her to Singapore. In 1975 she was laid up in Melsomvik (Norway) and briefly returned to trade in 1977. In November 1977 she was sold to Italian buyers and was renamed *Voluntas,* being sold again in 1986 and renamed *Artico,* still under the Italian flag. Sold on in 1987 to Sicula Oceanica Spa (SIOSA) without a change of name, but laid up in Brindisi, she was eventually sold for breaking up in Brindisi in May 1988.

And finally Trinity House and P. & A. Campbell

THV Alert, 1945, Trinity House

Swansea remains the only surviving outstation or depot for Trinity House-serving lighthouses and lightships that are still manned around the west coast. In the 1960s, Swansea was a major depot for Trinity House and there were at least six lightships needing support along the Bristol Channel so the resident tender was kept busy.

Alert was built at the end of the Second World War as the Admiralty cable-layer HMS *Bullseye*. Delivered after the war had ended, she was sold to Trinity House to replace an earlier *Alert* that had been mined and sunk off the coast of Normandy during the D-Day operations. A familiar sight, she was sold out of service in 1970.

THV Patricia, 1938, Trinity House

Built by Smith's Dock at Middlesbrough and equipped with diesel-electric machinery to aid manoeuvring, she was the largest of the tenders. She was virtually a yacht and was equipped with extra accommodation for use by committees, inspectors and VIPs. She represented Trinity House at major events and reviews. During the Second World War she had participated in the D-Day landings laying buoys.

Seen in the Prince of Wales Dock, she was probably filling in for the *Alert*. Replaced by a subsequent *Patricia*, it is believed she may still be in existence in Sweden.

Bristol Queen, 1946, 961 tons, P. & A. Campbell

The Campbell brothers had migrated from the River Clyde in 1887. They had previously operated steamers on the Clyde, but railway competition was slowly defeating the steamers. By 1922, their combination of experience and ability meant they were the sole operators of excursion steamers in the Bristol Channel.

A summertime delight in the 1950s and early 1960s was either a voyage across to Ilfracombe or a cruise along the Gower coast. One special delight was the evening cruise to the Scarweather lightship.

The *Bristol Queen* was built in Bristol by Charles Hill & Sons. For most of the post-war period, the services from Swansea were operated by the similar and slightly newer *Cardiff Queen*. That the *Bristol Queen* was in Swansea suggests that this photograph was taken in 1967, the year after the *Cardiff Queen* had been withdrawn. The *Bristol Queen* had been in collision with the pier at Penarth in August 1966, and sadly had to be withdrawn following a paddle wheel accident in August 1967. This was a tragedy. The two ships were fine vessels and relatively new. The *Bristol Queen* would have made a superb running mate for the preserved *Waverley*.

Although a screw steamer, the Paddle Steamer Preservation Society's *Balmoral* sports the traditional P. & A. Campbell white funnel colours.